CONSPIRACY IN THE STREETS

Also by Jon Wiener

Historians in Trouble:
Plagiarism, Fraud, and Politics in the Ivory Tower

Gimme Some Truth:
The John Lennon FBI Files

Professors, Politics, and Pop

Come Together: John Lennon in his Time

Social Origins of the New South

CONSPIRACY IN THE STREETS

The Extraordinary Trial of the Chicago Eight

Edited with an introduction
by Jon Wiener

THE NEW PRESS

NEW YORK
LONDON

Requests for permission to reproduce selections from this book
should be mailed to: Permissions Department,
The New Press, 38 Greene Street, New York, NY 10013

Published in the United States by The New Press, New York, 2006
Distributed by W. W. Norton & Company, Inc., New York

LIBRARY OF CONGRESS CATALOGING-IN-PUBLICATION DATA
Conspiracy in the streets : the extraordinary trial of the Chicago Eight /
edited with an introduction by Jon Wiener
p.   cm.
Includes bibliographical references.
ISBN-13: 978-1-56584-833-7 (pbk.)
ISBN-10: 1-56584-833-0 (pbk.)
1. Chicago Seven Trial, Chicago. Ill., 1969–1970.
2. Trials (Conspiracy)—Illinois—Chicago.
3. Riots—Illinois—Chicago.   I. Wiener, Jon.
KF224.C47W54   2006
345.773'1102—dc22   2005056185

The New Press was established in 1990 as a not-for-profit alternative
to the large, commercial publishing houses currently dominating the book
publishing industry. The New Press operates in the public
interest rather than for private gain, and is committed to publishing, in
innovative ways, works of educational, cultural, and community value that
are often deemed insufficiently profitable.

www.thenewpress.com

Book design and composition by dix!
This book was set in Bell MT Regular

Printed in the United States of America

2   4   6   8   10   9   7   5   3   1

The Conspiracy in the streets needs: freedom, actors, peace, turf, money, sunshine, musicians, instruments, people, props, cars, air, water, costumes, sound equipment, love, guns, freaks, friends, anarchy, Huey free, a truck, airplanes, power, glory, old clothes, space, truth, Nero, paint, paint, help, rope, swimming hole, ice cream, dope, nookie, moonship, Om, lords, health, no hassles, land, pigs, time, patriots, spacesuits, a Buick, people's justice, Eldridge, lumber, panthers, real things, good times.

—from a pamphlet distributed the week
before the Chicago Eight trial

Contents

List of Illustrations
by Jules Feiffer

Acknowledgments

This book was Colin Robinson's idea. He was wonderfully enthusiastic and effective in recruiting all the contributors and bringing the parts together. He got Jules Feiffer to let us use his drawings, and he got the Richard Avedon cover photo.

Tom Hayden read every word of both the edited trial transcript and the introduction—it was great to have a chance to work with him. Eric Foner provided encouragement at a crucial stage. Judy Fiskin provided astute and helpful comments and editing on many versions of the editor's introduction.

Turning a 22,000-page trial transcript into a 304-page book wasn't easy. Thanks to Adam Shatz, who edited a preliminary version of the trial transcript (before he became the literary editor of *The Nation*). We relied in part on the version of the trial transcript published in 1970 and edited by Judy Clavir—now Judy Albert—and John Spitzer, and we're grateful for their cooperation. The hardest work was done by Eileen Luhr, who checked our manuscript against the original trial transcript on microfilm and improved the final product in countless ways. Jules Feiffer generously provided the drawings he made at the time in the courtroom, and the estate of Richard Avedon allowed us use the gorgeous photo on the cover.

Laura Cadra, reference librarian at the Law Library at UCLA, provided the many reels of microfilm of the trial transcript and let us check them out. We also got help from Dean Rowan, reference librarian at the Boalt Hall Law Library at UC Berkeley. Dean Blobaum at the University of Chicago Press allowed us to publish a version of the magnificent Chicago Eight chronology on his website. We are grateful to the Humanities Center at UCI for a grant for manuscript preparation.

At The New Press, Sarah Fan did a terrific job managing the different parts of the book, and we had a great copy editor in Stuart Calderwood. Lizzie Seidlin-Bernstein solved many problems along the way.

Abbie and Jerry and Dave Dellinger are gone now, and so is Bill Kunstler—with this book we remember them.

Jon Wiener
Los Angeles
January 2006

Editor's Note

This is not a scholarly edition. The original trial transcript is 22,000 pages long; in cutting it down to 193 pages, we tried to select not only the most historically significant passages, but also some of the most dramatic confrontations and most amazing moments, in an effort to convey to readers the now-legendary aspects of the trial. We edited also to preserve some of the sheer human interest—the striking personalities and rhetorical styles of the central figures. Nevertheless, a lot is missing from the printed page, as law professor Harvey Kalven suggested: "the tone, the loudness, the sarcasm, the demeanor, the murmuring, and the degree of disturbance" in the courtroom. That is left for the reader to imagine.

In the interests of readability, we eliminated ellipses. Reading any trial transcript can be hard work; also in the interests of readability, "The Court" as a speaker has been changed to "Judge Hoffman," "Mr. Hoffman" has been changed to "Abbie Hoffman," and all the other speakers have been identified by first and last names, instead of "Mr." or "Miss," as they are in the original.

In producing this volume, we relied in part on the 600-page abridgment of the trial transcript published in 1970 by Bobbs-Merrill under the title *The Conspiracy Trial,* edited by Judy Clavir (now Judy Albert) and John Spitzer. We gratefully acknowledge their work and thank them for permission to make use of it. Readers interested in a fuller transcript should consult their volume, now out of print but widely available at libraries and used bookstores.

Those interested in the full version of the original 22,000-page transcript can find it on microfilm at law libraries at UCLA, NYU, and other places.

Jon Wiener

CONSPIRACY IN THE STREETS

Introduction
The Sixties on Trial

Jon Wiener

At the end of the sixties, it seemed that all the conflicts in America were distilled and then acted out in the courtroom of the Chicago Conspiracy trial. The trial focused on the demonstrations in Chicago in August 1968, where some 10,000 young people came to demonstrate outside the Democratic National Convention against the Vietnam War, to confront the warmakers in the name of the people. They were met by a similar number of policemen, National Guardsmen, and soldiers. The resulting battles, broadcast on national TV to an audience of millions, "marked a crisis in the nation's political and cultural order."[1] Eight months later, federal prosecutors indicted eight leaders and charged them with conspiracy and incitement to riot. The trial, which dominated the news for months, pushed the country to decide what they thought about the passions and commitments of the antiwar movement, and about the tactics and arguments of the defenders of the status quo.

In the courtroom, the accused confronted a judge and prosecutors who seemed to represent everything that was unjust and oppressive about the status quo. The defendants outraged the mainstream—and thrilled young people everywhere—by treating the judge with a kind of mockery and open defiance rarely seen in an American court. Abbie Hoffman blew kisses to the jury, appeared in court with Jerry Rubin wearing judicial robes, and insulted Judge Julius Hoffman in Yiddish (both Hoffmans were Jewish). In front of the jury, Dave Dellinger called the testimony of the deputy chief of police "bullshit." Black Panther Bobby Seale, deprived of his own attorney and denied repeated demands to represent himself, called the judge "a rotten racist pig" and a "fascist pig liar." [2]

Judge Julius Hoffman played the role of repressive government official to the hilt, especially in his order that Bobby Seale should be bound and gagged. The result, seen by millions on TV and in newspapers and magazines (in sketches because cameras were not permitted in courtrooms), was the horrifying spectacle of a black man in chains in an American courtroom, shouting through a gag to demand his rights.

This courtroom confrontation took place against the background of the continuing war in Vietnam, antiwar demonstrations on hundreds of campuses, riots and rebellions in urban ghettoes, and Nixon moving into the White House after eight years of Democratic rule.

For the prosecution, the trial was intended to rewrite the history of the demonstrations and the antiwar movement in general, to portray them not as legitimate efforts by citizens to end a war that was immoral and wrong, but rather as an illegal and violent conspiracy in which honest people were duped and manipulated by a few self-appointed leaders.

In fact the leaders put on trial by the Nixon administration came from different movements, with different ideas about what was wrong in America and different strategies of how to change things. Leaders from three different movements faced the prosecutors in Chicago: the cultural radicals, Abbie Hoffman and Jerry Rubin, leaders of the "Yippies"; the political radicals, Dave Dellinger, Tom Hayden, and Rennie Davis, leaders of the National Mobilization to End the War in Vietnam—"the Mobe"; and the black radicals, represented by Bobby Seale, chairman of the Black Panther Party.

CULTURAL RADICALS: THE YIPPIES

The cultural radicals, Abbie Hoffman and Jerry Rubin, were part of a youth revolt which defined "freedom" much more broadly than the political radicals did. The delegitimation of authority brought by the Vietnam War led to a rejection not just of that policy but of virtually all the values and priorities of the adult world. The counterculture rejected work and the pursuit of wealth in favor of play and the pursuit of pleasure; it rejected family life in favor of communal living; it embraced drugs as both recreation and road to enlightenment; it celebrated sexual freedom as an alternative to sexual repression. It brought a playful element into politics, as the Youth International Party, the Yippies, mobilized humor to challenge injustice and exploitation. Their most famous event took place at the New York Stock Exchange in 1967, where Abbie Hoffman threw dollar bills from the gallery onto the trading floor, bringing the market to a halt while traders scrambled to grab money. And the counterculture celebrated youth at gigantic rock festivals—Woodstock brought more than 400,000 young people together in upstate New York in August 1969 for a three-day festival that was completely peaceful and nonviolent. For Chicago in August 1968, the Yippies planned their own "festival of life" to challenge the "festival of death" they saw at the Democratic National Convention.

Abbie Hoffman, thirty-three at the time of the trial, was an immensely talented radical and rebel. A Brandeis graduate, he had worked in the civil rights and peace movements of the early sixties. He understood the power of the media and worked on tactics to subvert it. He told a 1967 press conference that the antiwar demonstration being planned for the Pentagon would be an "exorcism to cast out the evil spirits" and that a "flower power contingent" would surround the Pentagon and then make it "rise in the air."[3]

Abbie saw the courtroom as the ideal place to put into action his ideas about guerrilla theater. He was one of two defendants picked to appear as witnesses, and his testimony was brilliant and often hilarious:

Q: "Between the date of your birth November 30, 1936, and May 1, 1960, what if anything occurred in your life?"

A: "Nothing. I believe it is called an American education."[4]

Jerry Rubin, thirty years old at the start of the trial, grew up in a working-class Jewish family in Cincinnati and became a Berkeley student radical and a leader of the movement to stop troop trains in Oakland. He ran for mayor of Berkeley and received 22 percent of the vote. In 1966 he developed a radical media politics, winning headlines and news coverage for appearing before the feared House Un-American Activities Committee (HUAC), which was investigating the antiwar movement; Jerry wore a Revolutionary War uniform and passed out copies of the Declaration of Independence. He said he wanted to show young people "you didn't have to be scared, that you could turn your fear into courage." [5] It was his idea that the fall 1967 antiwar mobilization in Washington, D.C., should focus on the Pentagon, not the U.S. Capitol as demonstration leaders had originally planned.

BLACK RADICALS: THE PANTHERS

The civil rights movement had become more militant during the mid-sixties, as the era of "We Shall Overcome" gave way to "Black Power," a slogan first heard in 1966 among activists inspired by Malcolm X and embittered by the federal government's failure to stop attacks on civil rights workers in the Deep South. "Black Power" meant different things to different people; the most prominent new group raising the slogan was the Black Panther Party, founded in 1966 in Oakland by Huey Newton and Bobby Seale and best known for its advocacy of armed self-defense in response to police attacks. The Panthers' ten-point program included an end to police brutality, full employment, and the exemption of black men from military service. Unlike other black radical groups in the late sixties, the Panthers welcomed alliances with white radicals who shared their revolutionary goals, including Students for a Democratic Society (SDS) and later the Weather Underground. The Panthers ran breakfast programs for poor children, but thirty of them also demonstrated their beliefs by marching onto the floor of the California legislature carrying guns. Bobby Seale read a statement and then was arrested, along with the other Panthers.

Bobby Seale, chairman of the Black Panther Party, thirty-three years old at the time of the trial, had the public persona of a fierce advocate of armed self-defense. "The real Bobby," Tom Hayden later wrote, "was an angry and inflammatory person, to be sure, but he also exuded a humanity, keen powers of observation, a sense of humor, and a desire for simple decency behind his mask. Not all the Panthers were as responsible as Bobby."[6]

The year before the Chicago demonstrations and the trial, black militants like the Panthers had a worldview that was completely different from that of the counterculture. For America's hippies, 1967 was the "summer of love," a time when "flower children" flocked to festivals and parks to sing "All You Need Is Love," the Beatles song that was a number-one hit that summer. For black America, however, that was "the long, hot summer" when ghetto uprisings, rebellions, and insurrections left thousands arrested and injured and dozens killed, especially in Newark and Detroit.

This distance between white and black youth made the indictment of Bobby Seale as part of the Chicago Conspiracy all the more unlikely. The Panthers had no interest in protesting against the Democratic Party in 1968; Seale had never met Abbie Hoffman, Jerry Rubin, or any of the other defendants except Tom Hayden before the trial; Seale had had nothing to do with planning the demonstrations and had given only one speech in Chicago. But the Nixon administration was interested in the Panthers, in prosecuting and jailing their leaders, as part of their repressive "law and order" politics; so Seale was indicted as a member of the Chicago Conspiracy.

POLITICAL RADICALS: THE "MOBE"

In addition to the cultural radicals and the black radicals, the third group put on trial in Chicago were the political radicals, represented by Dave Dellinger, Rennie Davis, and Tom Hayden.

Dave Dellinger, at fifty-four, was the oldest of the defendants, and a lifelong Christian socialist and pacifist. The son of a wealthy lawyer, Dellinger went to Yale and Oxford—and then, during World War II, he went to prison for three years as a pacifist and conscientious objector. He opposed the Korean War and then in the mid-sixties became the chairman of the National Mobilization Committee to End the War in Vietnam—"the Mobe." J. Anthony Lukas, who covered the trial for the *New York Times*, wrote that "he looked like an off-duty scoutmaster."[7]

Rennie Davis, twenty-nine at the time of the trial, was a wholesome all-American type who testified that he first came to Chicago as a kid for an agricultural youth club chicken-raising contest, where he won fourth place. An Oberlin graduate, by the mid-sixties he became the New Left's most talented organizer. In the leadership of the Mobe, according to Lukas, "he did most of the real organizing" for both the demonstrations and then the trial.[8] He visited North Vietnam in 1967. The defense picked him as one of two who would appear on the witness stand.

Tom Hayden was also twenty-nine at the time of the trial; Lukas wrote that, of all the defendants, he had the most "sheer intelligence."[9] Raised as a middle-class Irish Catholic in Michigan, he graduated from the University of Michigan and was one of the founders of Students for a Democratic Society (SDS). He worked with civil rights activists in the South in

1961 and was beaten by a white mob in McComb, Mississippi. The next year he drafted the "Port Huron Statement" for SDS, stating the ideals and goals of the New Left.[10] He organized poor people in Newark for three years, and he witnessed the weeklong rebellion of July 1967. He also traveled to North Vietnam in 1965. He was a key strategist for the Mobe and the national movement, and more than any of the other defendants wanted a defense strategy that would not simply defy the court but also win over some jurors and result in a hung jury— permitting the defendants to continue their antiwar work instead of going to jail.

Two others were indicted: John Froines and Lee Weiner. Froines was a young PhD chemist; Weiner was a PhD student in sociology at Northwestern. They had been marshals at the Chicago demonstrations but were not national leaders and indeed at the end of the trial were found not guilty of all charges.

THE WAR AND THE TRIAL

The prosecution and the judge insisted that the trial was about conspiracy and incitement to riot; the defense insisted that the trial was about the war and the right to demonstrate against it. The official version of the war portrayed it as an effort to defend democracy in a country being invaded by Communists acting on behalf of the Soviet Union and China. The defendants saw the war essentially as a continuation of the Vietnamese fight for independence, which began as a fight against French colonialism after World War II. That phase ended in 1954 with the Vietnamese victory and the Geneva Accords, the peace treaty that divided Vietnam into two zones, the Communist North and the U.S.-backed South. Under the Geneva Accords, elections and reunification were promised within two years.

The defendants often noted that South Vietnam was not a democracy and that democracy had been blocked in Vietnam in 1956, when President Eisenhower stopped the elections because it was clear that the Communists would win—after all, they had led the independence struggle. At this point the United States began sending military forces to defend the Saigon government it had established. The defendants often noted that the Democrats were more responsible for the war than were the Republicans: Kennedy had sent 16,000 American "advisers." Lyndon Johnson brought a massive escalation: at the time of the Democratic Convention in Chicago, the United States had half a million soldiers fighting the Vietnamese and had dropped more tons of bombs on the small country of Vietnam than both sides dropped in all of World War II.

The defendants had been organizing against the war for four or five years when they were put on trial. Most of them had been part of the first antiwar march on Washington, organized by SDS in April 1965—about 25,000 people took part, surprising everyone, including the organizers. In 1967 SDS had 30,000 members in 247 chapters, ranging from Harvard, Yale, and Princeton to working-class community colleges. As the war got bigger and more destructive, SDS escalated its rhetoric and strategy, urging young men to burn their draft cards and refuse to serve in the military—and thousands did. In October 1967 the movement reached a new peak of numbers and impact with the dramatic and massive march on the Pentagon. That demonstration inspired the idea of a march on the Democratic National Convention, which was to be held in Chicago the following year. By 1968, SDS was calling for a move "from protest to resistance."

1968 marked the climax of the sixties; the protests in Chicago at the Democratic National Convention followed seven months of events that shattered the way most Americans understood their world. First of all came the war: American officials had regularly declared that the tide was turning and that they could see light at the end of the tunnel. But in late January 1968, the Communists launched the Tet Offensive, simultaneous surprise attacks on every city and provincial capital in South Vietnam, which culminated with their fighters penetrating the American embassy compound in the heart of Saigon. The Tet Offensive convinced Americans that they couldn't believe their leaders, and that the Vietnam War could not be won. But still the war continued; the death toll by the time of the convention protests in August 1968 was almost 30,000 Americans and hundreds of thousands of Vietnamese.[11]

LBJ, facing a reelection campaign in 1968, had been challenged in the Democratic primaries by Senator Eugene McCarthy of Minnesota. After LBJ withdrew from his own reelection campaign at the end of March, Robert Kennedy, then a senator from New York, entered the primaries as a second antiwar candidate, and Vice President Hubert Humphrey became the candidate of the party regulars. The Chicago convention, it appeared, would see a real choice over the candidate, the war, and the future of the Democrats.

Then in April came the assassination in Memphis of Martin Luther King—by a white man—provoking the biggest wave of black riots and rebellions in American history. In Chicago, Mayor Richard Daley issued orders to the police to "shoot to kill" arsonists and "shoot to maim or cripple" looters in black neighborhoods—this was only four months before Mayor Daley confronted demonstrators at the Democratic National Convention, and protest leaders worried about Daley's stance on "violence in the streets."

The nation suffered a second immense blow in June, when Robert Kennedy was assassinated in Los Angeles by a Palestinian nationalist on the night of the California primary.

Meanwhile Richard Nixon returned to the American political stage—Nixon, who had failed to win election as California governor in 1962, six years earlier, after his term ended as Eisenhower's vice president. Nixon based his presidential campaign on mobilizing a backlash against the sixties, calling on "the silent majority"—code words for conservative whites—to stand up for "law and order"—code words for opposition to militant blacks and antiwar students.

WHAT HAPPENED IN CHICAGO

The eight defendants were charged with conspiring to riot in the streets of Chicago. But in the months before the convention, the leaders had done their best to make the upcoming protests legal and peaceful. Both the Yippies and the Mobe applied to the city of Chicago for permits to demonstrate. The city turned them down. They went to court asking for permits. The court turned them down. With no permits, there would be no electricity for a stage for the bands, and thus no "festival of life"—virtually guaranteeing a violent confrontation between police and protesters.

The commission charged with investigating the events outside the Democratic National Convention in Chicago later described what happened as a "police riot." Those events were scrutinized in exhaustive detail during the trial. Briefly:

Sunday, August 25, 1968: The day before the official opening of the Convention. Demonstrators and activists began gathering in Lincoln Park. The city had decreed an 11 P.M. curfew for the park. On the first night of demonstrations, Tom Hayden and Rennie Davis led a march from the park to the Conrad Hilton Hotel, the main hotel for convention delegates. At midnight, police enforced the curfew, attacking people in the park with tear gas and clubs and arresting them; thousands fled through the streets.

Monday, August 26: First day of the convention. Abbie Hoffman and Jerry Rubin urged demonstrators to hold the park. Tom Hayden was arrested in the afternoon, then was bailed out. At 11 P.M., the hour of the curfew, about 3,000 people in the park were attacked by police shooting not only tear gas but also blanks from shotguns. Tom Hayden was arrested for a second time, jailed, then bailed out.[12]

Tuesday, August 27: At sunrise, poet Allen Ginsberg led protesters in chanting, prayers, and meditation. Opponents of the war held a rally at the Chicago Coliseum, an indoor space where some 4,000 protesters heard speeches by Dave Dellinger, Abbie Hoffman, and others, and music by Phil Ochs and others. In Lincoln Park, Bobby Seale gave a speech to about 2,000. At 11 P.M. police charged and clubbed people in the park. Some demonstrators responded by spreading out in the neighborhood to trash store windows and fight running battles with the police.

Wednesday, August 28: A force of about 12,000 police, 6,000 soldiers, and 5,000 National Guardsmen was mobilized, while at Grant Park, a rally of more than 15,000 protesters, the largest of the convention, met at noon at the bandshell, not far from the Hilton. During the speeches, one teenaged guy climbed the flagpole; the police charged through the audience to stop him, clubbing and gassing people. Rennie Davis was beaten badly by police and hospitalized. Allen Ginsberg and Dick Gregory spoke. Dave Dellinger tried to lead a march to the Amphitheatre, but the police blocked it. Elsewhere in the area, police attacked demonstrators with clubs and tear gas. The battles continued into the evening, when the network TV coverage of the convention nominating Humphrey was interrupted by live scenes of thousands of police clubbing demonstrators.

Inside the convention hall, Senator Abraham Ribicoff, a Democrat from Connecticut, speaking from the floor in opposition to Humphrey, denounced what he called "Gestapo tactics on the streets of Chicago." Mayor Daley was shown on national TV shouting back at Senator Ribicoff; his voice was inaudible, but lip-readers saw him yelling "Fuck you, you Jew son-of-a-bitch, you lousy mother-fucker, go home."[13] Tom Hayden and other demonstrators outside the Hilton were pushed through broken plate-glass windows; police charged into the hotel, turning the lounge and lobby into a battleground. The convention officially came to an end.

Of course Nixon ended up winning on election day in November, but by the smallest of margins: about 600,000 votes out of 70 million. He got only 43 percent of the popular vote, because the Deep South was carried by third-party candidate George Wallace, who appealed to Southern white racists. Humphrey probably would have won, historians argue, if he had come out against the war before the end of the campaign.[14]

THE INDICTMENTS, THE ATTORNEYS, THE JUDGE, AND THE JURY

Nixon was inaugurated on January 20, 1969. The Chicago Eight were indicted two months later on March 20. All eight were charged with conspiracy to travel interstate "with the intent to incite, organize, promote, encourage, participate in, and carry out a riot." Dellinger, Hayden, Davis, Hoffman, Rubin, and Seale were also charged with inciting violence. Each of the two charges carried a five-year sentence; each defendant thus faced a ten-year prison term. Froines and Weiner were not charged with inciting violence, but with teaching others how to make "incendiary devices."

The other central figures in the trial included defense attorney William Kunstler, fifty years old, a dramatic courtroom figure who had argued many civil rights cases in the South. He had represented Martin Luther King Jr. and Black Panthers Stokely Carmichael and H. Rap Brown, as well as Malcolm X. He had impressive rhetorical skills and an awesome ability to respond quickly to events in the courtroom.

Leonard Weinglass, the second defense attorney, had never tried a case in federal court before. Tom Hayden brought him into the defense because they had been friends since Tom worked in Newark and Len taught nearby at Rutgers. He turned out to be a brilliant lawyer, a master of the material as well as a tireless worker.

Judge Julius Hoffman came to personify for the movement everything unjust and punitive about the establishment. At the time of the trial he was old—seventy-four. He had been born in Chicago, and graduated from law school way back in 1915. He had become a local judge in 1947 and a federal district judge in 1953, sponsored by a Republican senator. He was a member of several exclusive clubs and lived in an upper-class neighborhood of Chicago. During the trial he objected bitterly to being called a racist by Bobby Seale and others, often recalling for the record that he issued the first court order for school desegregation in the North the year before the trial. But his rhetoric came from an earlier era: "If there's any judge on the bench who looks after underprivileged members of other races," he told one lawyer, "it's me." He also resented it when Abbie Hoffman brought up the fact that Judge Hoffman was Jewish—part of the German-Jewish elite of Chicago. J. Anthony Lukas of the *New York Times* wondered "whether the judge's efforts to escape his own Jewishness might not explain some of what went on in that courtroom"—in particular his hard-to-explain rage at the Jews who misbehaved—Kunstler, Weinglass, Weiner, Rubin, and Hoffman.[15]

The two government attorneys played contrasting roles: the senior one, Thomas Foran, was the calm professional, while his assistant, Richard Schultz, spoke in a voice of perpetual outrage. As U.S. attorney Foran had gone after organized crime in

Chicago with a vengeance. He claimed to have been a friend of Robert Kennedy. His closest political mentor was Mayor Daley, who told the jury that Foran was "one of the greatest attorneys in this country and the finest man I have met in private and public life." Richard Schultz was younger and less experienced but proud of his mastery of the details of the case. Schultz seemed to believe that there really had been a conspiracy—Lukas wrote that "Schultz could have made the first robin of spring sound like a plot by the Audubon Society." [16]

The jury suffered every day of the trial. The judge ordered them sequestered on the first day, which meant that at the end of each day's testimony they were taken directly to the Palmer House hotel and prevented by the federal marshals from having any contact with the outer world. They were not allowed to read newspapers or magazines or watch TV. Instead, the marshals selected movies for them to watch—as a group—every Friday and Saturday night: all the James Bond films, and harmless musicals like *Oklahoma!* and *The Music Man*.

While the jury was locked up at the Palmer House, the defendants went out almost every night to give speeches, raise money, and turn the trial into a tool for more antiwar organizing.

LEGAL ISSUES: CONSPIRACY

The first charge in the indictment was "conspiracy," a charge that prosecutors typically like, but which on its face seems problematic. [17] Under the law, a person can be charged not only with committing a crime, but with agreeing with two or more other people to commit the same crime. That would seem to be a kind of double jeopardy—two convictions for the same offense. Moreover, under conspiracy law, prosecutors do not have to convince a jury that the actual crime occurred for the conspiracy itself to be punishable. In modern American history, conspiracy laws had been used both against trade unions planning strikes and against corporate officials planning to fix prices. Probably the most dramatic conspiracy trial in American history at the time of the Chicago trial was the conviction of Julius and Ethel Rosenberg in 1951, not for having stolen the secret of the atom bomb, but for having conspired to do it. Prosecutors like conspiracy law also because each member of a conspiracy is responsible for the entire conspiracy, for all the actions and words of the other conspirators. In the Chicago case, the conspiracy charge permitted the government to bring together many leaders of the antiwar movement in one big, dramatic trial. Without the conspiracy charge, each would be entitled to a separate trial on the other charges.

In fact the defense had strong evidence that no conspiracy to riot had ever existed. A key planning document drafted by Tom Hayden and Rennie Davis in March 1968, five months before the demonstrations, read in part that "the campaign should not plan violence and disruption against the Democratic convention. It should be nonviolent and legal. . . . any plan of deliberate disruption will drive away people who are worried about arrests or violence, and thus sharply diminish the size and political effect of the mobilization."[18] The judge refused to allow the jury to learn of this existence of this document. Nevertheless the jury in the end agreed with the defense, and

on the conspiracy charges brought in a verdict for each of the
defendants of "Not Guilty."

LEGAL ISSUES: INTENT TO INCITE

Six of the defendants were charged not only with conspiracy
but also with crossing state lines with the intent of starting a
riot. This federal crime was brand-new at the time, and its passage reveals much about the context of the trial. The law had
been passed in 1968 and was called "the Rap Brown law."
Brown, chairman of the Student Nonviolent Coordinating
Committee in the summer of 1967, had given a speech to several hundred people in Cambridge, Maryland, where he said,
"It's time for Cambridge to explode, baby. Black folks built
America, and if America don't come around, we're going to
burn America down." An hour later, police exchanged gunfire
with black residents, and several hours later, fires destroyed
most of the city's black-owned business district as well as a
black public school.[19]

In that famously hot summer of 1967, riots had already
broken out in black ghettoes in a dozen American cities, most
of all in Newark and Detroit, where what happened was more
like an uprising or an insurrection. In each city, the burning
and looting was triggered not by "outside agitators" but rather
by actions of the local police. In Newark the governor sent in
about 17,500 National Guardsmen, untrained and poorly prepared, who shot black people indiscriminately and also destroyed black-owned stores that had been spared by the rioters.
Tom Hayden was a community organizer in Newark at the

time; the governor asked him what to do, and his advice was straightforward: withdraw the National Guard. The governor took Hayden's advice, but twenty-three people had been killed—twenty-one of whom were blacks, mostly innocent by-standers killed by Guardsmen or police. Meanwhile, in Detroit, another uprising resulted in fires that destroyed almost one hundred square blocks of the black ghetto; the governor said "it looked like the city had been bombed." [20] The death toll there was thirty-three blacks and ten whites.

Rap Brown gave his speech in Cambridge, Maryland, one week after Detroit: "Don't be trying to love that honky to death," he declared, standing on the trunk of a car. "Shoot him to death. Shoot him to death, brother, because that's what he is out to do to you. Do to him like he would do to you, but do it to him first." [21]

Even then Rap Brown might not have become the catalyst for a new federal antiriot law—but Maryland's Republican governor, a relative unknown named Spiro Agnew, declared the next day, "It shall now be the policy of this state to immediately arrest any person inciting to riot, and to not allow that person to finish his vicious speech." Agnew had been elected as a moderate who had significant support from liberals and blacks. But his new hard-line rhetoric propelled him to instant national prominence, won him the vice-presidential spot at the Republican convention a year later, and set a new political agenda for Republicans: win white votes with "tough" rhetoric against black militants. [22]

Southern whites in Congress took the lead in calling for a federal antiriot law. These Congressmen blamed all civil rights activism on "outside agitators," as in the frequently heard argument "our nigras were doin' jes' fine until these outside agita-tors showed up." Of course the number-one "outside agitator" in America in 1967 was Martin Luther King Jr. This was the era when the Solid South was a Democratic bastion (indeed 1968 marks the turning point in the shift of Southern whites from Democratic to Republican, by way of the George Wallace third-party campaign of 1968).

In Congress the House passed a federal antiriot bill in Feb-ruary 1967, opposed by Northern liberals on the grounds that it was an unconstitutional violation of freedom of speech and assembly. LBJ's attorney general, Ramsey Clark, opposed it publicly in the summer of 1967, arguing that state laws were adequate and that "outside agitators" in fact were "not directly responsible or even indirectly responsible for these riots."[23] President Johnson in his January 1968 State of the Union speech declared he would not support federal antiriot legisla-tion, and the Senate failed to pass the House bill.

But a month later Johnson reversed himself, hoping to head off "law-and-order" Republican opposition to his ex-pected run for reelection that fall. He also needed the support of Southern Democrats for the increasingly unpopular war in Vietnam. Here the pact with the devil was hatched. Senate lib-erals had been pushing for a new civil rights act, which would feature an open-housing section, making it a federal crime for some property owners to refuse to sell to black people. But the bill had been bogged down by the threat of a filibuster by Southern Democrats. Senator Strom Thurmond of South Car-olina introduced an antiriot bill as an amendment to the civil rights bill. Now the only way to defeat the filibuster and get the Civil Rights Act of 1968 into law was to accept an antiriot amendment as part of the bill.

So the Senate passed the Civil Rights Act of 1968 with the antiriot provision. The Senate's leading liberals voted in favor: Robert Kennedy, Ted Kennedy, George McGovern, and others. In congratulating themselves, they failed to mention the antiriot part of the bill. Southern Democrats all voted against it because of the open-housing provision. Johnson signed it into law on April 11, saying nothing about the antiriot bill. His justice department, headed by Ramsey Clark, did not bring any antiriot indictments.

The law was hypocritical because it promised to "do something" about the riots sweeping America's black ghettoes—but, as Ramsey Clark had argued, those riots were not caused by the famed "outside agitators" crossing state lines to instigate violence. The uprisings in Newark and Detroit, and in Watts before them, were very much homegrown events in which black communities responded to local police provocations. H. Rap Brown's speech in Cambridge, Maryland was the exception.

Nine months after the antiriot law was passed, Nixon was elected; eleven months later, a federal grand jury in Chicago issued the first indictments under the antiriot provisions of the Civil Rights Act of 1968. Those indicted were not black militants like H. Rap Brown charged with inciting ghetto rebellions, but rather five antiwar leaders of the Chicago convention protests (plus Bobby Seale, charged for the same antiwar demonstrations). Congressman William Cramer of Florida spoke in the House: "As author of the antiriot act, I naturally had been concerned over the apparent recalcitrance of the previous attorney general to enforce its provisions," he said. "I commend the President and Attorney General Mitchell for implementing the first essential step toward restoring tranquility in the United States."[24]

LEGAL ISSUES: RAMSEY CLARK'S LIST OF FAILURES

If Humphrey had been elected in November 1968, there would have been no Chicago Conspiracy trial—that's what LBJ's attorney general Ramsey Clark said. Clark called the trial transcript "a record of torment."[25] He left office when Nixon was inaugurated on January 20, 1969. Clark was no peacenik; at the time he was a mainstream liberal. He had indicted and prosecuted antiwar leaders, including Dr. Benjamin Spock, for "conspiracy to aid and abet draft resistance." (He also presided over the most far-reaching federal action in support of civil rights in a century, including the Voting Rights Act of 1965.) At the Chicago trial, he was called as a witness for the defense, which hoped to have him tell the jury why he opposed the indictments. But Judge Hoffman refused to allow the jury to hear his testimony.

He subsequently described the Chicago trial as one that "failed miserably" and urged Americans to learn the lessons of the trial "to avoid its mistakes" in the future. His list of failures is a long one, starting with the law creating a new federal crime, the crime of crossing state lines with the intent to incite a riot. It was a law whose "genesis," he suggested, was "only fear and hypocrisy": state laws against incitement and rioting should have been sufficient, he suggested, if a crime indeed had been committed in Chicago by the demonstration organizers.[26]

The second failure Clark described came at the beginning: the refusal of Chicago authorities to issue permits so that people opposed to the war could gather, hear speeches, march, and demonstrate at the Democratic convention. Clearly opponents of the war had a First Amendment right to assemble to speak out against the war. Of course it's possible that some demonstrators would have committed violent acts even if permits had been issued, but almost certainly the great majority would not have.

The third failure Clark pointed to was official sanction for a police riot. Strong leadership in the city—which is to say, Mayor Daley—should have made it clear that police discipline was required and that lawbreaking by the police would not be tolerated. Instead Mayor Daley gave police the opposite message.

The conspiracy charge should never have been brought, Clark suggested. Any prosecution should have focused on illegal acts of violence and incitement. Indeed the acquittal of all the defendants on the conspiracy charge suggested to Clark that conspiracy was simply a prosecution ploy to permit all the defendants to be brought together for a single show trial, instead of holding eight separate trials.

Clark suggested also that Bobby Seale should never have been indicted. He had nothing to do with planning the protest, attended only at the last minute, and gave a brief speech in which he said the same thing he and many other black militants had said "thousands of times" without being prosecuted.[27]

It was also a failure, Clark suggested, to put the case in the hands of a federal prosecutor closely identified with the mayor, a prosecutor who had been personally involved in the events at issue. Finally, assigning the case to Judge Hoffman was a mistake, in Clark's view. He was not "temperamentally suited" to a trial of such "inherent volatility."[28]

The fact that the attorney general of the previous Democratic administration had decided not to indict the Chicago demonstration leaders, that he publicly criticized the indictments and the trial, and that he was prepared to testify for the defense, underlines the fact that this really was a political trial from the start.

LEGAL ISSUES: THE DEFENSE STRATEGY

The defense approached the trial as a rich opportunity for making the antiwar argument before a national audience. They planned to go beyond disputing the facts described in the indictment, and, as Tom Hayden later wrote, present to the jury and the country their understanding of "what was going on in America that motivated us to take a stand in Chicago." [29] They wanted to argue that the trial was an attempt by the government to divert attention from the war, and they wanted to assert an American "right of resistance." Their strategy was part of the move from protest to resistance; they wanted to take resistance into the courtroom, to mock the system and thereby delegitimize it, to use the trial to rally antiwar forces across the country, and inside the courtroom to appeal to the jury with the radical doctrine of jury nullification—the notion that the jury can judge the law as well as the evidence, that the jury can conclude the law was unjust, and set the defendants free.

Beyond this, in pretrial meetings the defendants were divided about their strategy. They disagreed on whether to try to win over a couple of jurors with deliberate, rational arguments and thus end up with a hung jury that would avoid "guilty" verdicts and keep the defendants out of jail and organizing against the war—this was Hayden's position. The alternative strategy was to disrupt, defy, and thus "desanctify" the court for the larger audience outside—this the view of the Yippies, of Abbie Hoffman and Jerry Rubin, and also of Dave Dellinger. Rennie Davis brokered a compromise where both antiwar politics and youth-culture theater would be presented—a total of 104 witnesses for the defense who together would personify the history of the sixties.

UNDERSTANDING THE VERDICT

The defense strategy failed to hang the jury; in the end, all twelve jurors agreed to convict five defendants on the incitement charge. All defendants were found not guilty on the other charges. Why did all twelve jurors agree? One later told her story to the *Chicago Sun-Times* for several thousand dollars. She explained that four jurors had been won over by the defense, and had favored "not guilty" verdicts on all charges. In their deliberations the jury argued for four days. Twice they told the judge they were hopelessly deadlocked and could not reach a verdict—which would have resulted in no guilty verdicts if the judge had accepted their statement. But, as one of the jurors who favored "not guilty" verdicts later told Tom Hayden, "the marshal came back in, saying 'you have to keep deliberating.' "[30]

"We couldn't understand the indictment," Kay Richards wrote—she was one of the jurors who favored convictions. "We didn't really know what the charges were." Instead of judging the evidence according to the law, the twelve jurors divided into eight who believed punishment was the right way to deal with rebellious troublemakers, and four who disagreed. One in the first group later told the press, "These defendants wouldn't even stand up when the judge walked in. When there's no more respect, we might as well give up on the United states." [31] That certainly wasn't what they were on trial for.

A "compromise" verdict was what they finally agreed to, organized by Kay Richards; "the trial had to come to some kind of conclusion just to prove that it works," she later said. "It hurts people but it works." Of course the jury did not have an obligation to prove the system worked. Jean Fritz, who initially favored "not guilty" verdicts, later told Hayden that she and her three allies couldn't sleep and finally "became hysterical and collapsed" before they agreed to the "compromise." After the verdicts were read and the jury was dismissed, "I went to pieces," she told Hayden. "I started to cry, and I couldn't stop. I kept saying over and over again, 'I just voted five men guilty on speeches I don't even remember.' " [32] So the prosecution strategy behind the otherwise puzzling indictments succeeded: Give the jury a variety of defendants and charges so that, if the jury was divided, they could "compromise" with some innocent verdicts and some guilty.

At the end of the trial, Judge Hoffman sentenced each of the five "guilty" defendants to five years in prison plus a $5,000 fine. Each was also sentenced to a jail term for contempt of court, as were their two attorneys. All were freed on bond pending appeal.

AFTER THE TRIAL: THE APPEAL

The appeals court in November 1972 overturned all the convictions. First the court ruled that the judge was wrong to reject the jury's messages that they were unable to agree on any verdicts. That alone was "grounds for reversal." The appeals court also ruled that the judge had been systematically biased against the defense, and that the prosecution had broken the rules in its summation—both of which were grounds for reversal. And since the jury had rejected the conspiracy charge, if the government wanted to retry the defendants, they were entitled to separate trials. In any retrial, Attorney General Ramsey Clark would be permitted to testify.[33] The government elected not to retry any of the defendants.

The appeals court also ordered a new trial on the contempt charges, which convened in Chicago in October 1973, three and a half years after the original trial ended. Judge Hoffman had sentenced all eight of the original defendants and their two attorneys for a total of 175 incidents of contempt. The contempt sentences totaled more than nineteen years; the individual sentences ranged from two and a half months (Weiner) to more than four years (Seale and Kunstler). Judge Hoffman had ordered that the sentences for contempt run concurrently with the sentences on the original charges, so in practice only Froines and Weiner, who had been found not guilty on all charges, and Kunstler and Weinglass faced actual jail time for contempt.[34]

The Supreme Court's rules for contempt cases held that a separate jury trial, with a separate judge, was required in cases where "serious" penalties were possible—and "serious" had come to be defined as sentences of more than six months. Judge Hoffman had carefully and exhaustively listed each incident of contempt and declared a specific penalty. Many of them appeared frivolous—for blowing a kiss to the jury (Abbie Hoffman), one day in jail; for laughing in court, seven days. Were these really crimes deserving of prison sentences? Normally in a contempt case the entire trial record was submitted, rather than separate incidents, and a single sentence issued. Apparently Judge Hoffman had hoped that by issuing separate sentences for separate acts, where each of the sentences were less than six months, he could avoid the requirement of a separate trial. So even though Kunstler and Seale received sentences of more than four years, no single offense merited more than six months.

The political context in which the contempt charges were retried was strikingly different from the original trial. Nixon had been reelected in a landslide in November 1972; George McGovern carried only Massachusetts. Nixon had campaigned saying he had "a secret plan to end the war," which nevertheless continued. In December 1972, Nixon ordered the Christmas bombing of Hanoi—the most brutal and destructive of the war—which was met with outrage by the antiwar movement at home and widespread opposition abroad. It failed to budge the North Vietnamese position in the secret peace talks that had been under way.

The U.S. war in Vietnam came to an end in January 1973 with a treaty that conceded defeat. In the Paris Peace Agreement, the United States agreed to withdraw all its troops within sixty days, and it accepted the presence of North Vietnamese troops in the South. It preserved the fiction that the Saigon government was an independent ally of the United States; in exchange, North Vietnam agreed to release the POWs who had been captured when B-52s had been shot down. Meanwhile the *Washington Post* started publishing articles by Bob Woodward and Carl Bernstein about Watergate. It was at this point that a new judge began a new trial on the contempt charges.

In the conventional view, the contempt exhibited in the courtroom was part of a deliberate strategy of the defense to disrupt the trial, to bring the confrontation from the streets into the courtroom. The incidents Judge Hoffman cited in his contempt citations in this view had been intended by the defendants to "delegitimize the system." Some of the defendants said as much during and after the trial. But a careful study of the contempt citations shows that this was not the case. Harry Kalven, a law professor at the University of Chicago who studied the contempt charges, concluded that most of the incidents took place on only sixteen days—during a trial that lasted for five months. Long stretches, weeks at a time, had virtually no incidents of contempt. In fact all the serious incidents that Judge Hoffman cited as contempt were triggered by two or three events: the treatment of Bobby Seale, first denying him the right to represent himself and then the intolerable spectacle of him bound and gagged; and then the revoking of Dave Dellinger's bond and sending him, the oldest and most respected of the defendants, to jail late in the trial. Kalven concludes that the defense did not pursue a consistent strategy of disrupting the trial process, but instead protested at specific events which seemed outrageous and unjust not only to the defendants but to many observers.[35]

The retrial on the contempt charges took place before a new judge, Edward Gignoux of Maine. After five weeks, he ruled that 146 of Judge Hoffman's 159 citations were not valid. He declared each could "be said to have been in response, albeit an excessive response, to peremptory action by the judge."

Only thirteen of the citations were upheld. Tom Hayden and Rennie Davis were cleared of all contempt charges, as were John Froines, Lee Weiner, and attorney Leonard Weinglass. Four were found guilty of some contempt—Jerry Rubin, Abbie Hoffman, Dave Dellinger, and attorney William Kunstler—but the judge decided not to impose any jail sentences, on the grounds that the time they had already spent in jail was sufficient punishment.

AFTER THE TRIAL: THE DEFENDANTS[36]

ABBIE HOFFMAN's life after the trial was in some ways even more amazing than his life before the trial. In 1971 he published *Steal This Book*, a guide to living for free, outside the law, in America—it described an era, in his biographer Jonah Raskin's words, "when it was still possible for dropouts from suburbia to find a more or less comfortable "crash pad" in a strange city, get on welfare and obtain food stamps with relative ease." Tens of thousands of copies were bought (or stolen). But as the movement fell apart, Abbie became a cocaine dealer, and in August 1973 he was arrested in a New York City hotel, making front-page news in the city, and shocking his old movement friends and fans. He faced a sentence of fifteen years to life in prison. Bailed out with the help of a defense committee that included Norman Mailer, Abbie decided to jump bail and go underground in the winter of 1974. In his underground life, he had plenty of money, but he faced growing problems of depression. In his 1980 memoir titled *Soon to Be a Major Motion Picture*, he described "psychotic" episodes when "I craved death but lacked the energy or initiative to do the deed. . . . Every day began with thoughts of suicide and turning myself in." [37]

He was saved from suicide in the seventies, according to Raskin, by returning to political activism—with a new identity. "Barry Freed," a dynamo of an organizer for a community environmental organization called "Save the River" on the St. Lawrence River in upstate New York. He led delegations first to the state capitol in Albany, and in 1979 to Washington, D.C., to visit their local congressman. Senator Daniel Patrick Moynihan posed for pictures with him and told the press, "Everyone in New York State owes Barry Freed a debt of gratitude for his organizing ability." Increasingly eager to turn himself in, he engineered an interview with Barbara Walters on ABC's 20/20 where he came out as Abbie. Walters was completely won over and, according to Raskin, "turned the program into a vehicle for his cause." [38]

So on September 4, 1980, in front of a hundred reporters and photographers in New York City, Abbie turned himself in. He'd been underground for six-and-a-half years. He was granted bail, and pled guilty to possession of cocaine in exchange for the prosecution dropping charges of selling cocaine and jumping bail. He served two miserable months at a minimum-security prison, then was let out into a work-release program in Manhattan.

Before going to prison he had privately sought treatment for depression. Doctors diagnosed him as a manic-depressive with bipolar disorder and prescribed lithium. Once in a while he talked about being a manic-depressive, but he didn't take his medication consistently. He was rescued from one suicide attempt in the winter of 1983, and then went back to political ac-

tivism in the late eighties—most famously getting arrested in
1985, protesting CIA recruitment at the University of Massachusetts, along with Amy Carter, the ex-president's daughter.
Now he was a famous media figure and celebrity, with friends
in Hollywood and in TV; former President Carter said, "Abbie
Hoffman is a folk hero." [39]

But the crushing depression came back in 1988, when he
was living in Bucks County, Pennsylvania; he began preparing
again to commit suicide, Raskin reports, arranging his affairs
and making his farewells. On April 4, 1989, he appeared at Van-
derbilt University in Tennessee with Timothy Leary and
Bobby Seale. It would be his last public appearance, and Raskin
says "he planned it that way." He talked about the sixties: "We
were young, we were reckless, arrogant, silly, headstrong—and
we were right," he said. "I regret nothing. We ended legal segregation. . . . We ended the idea that you can send a million soldiers ten thousand miles away to fight in a war that people do
not support. We ended the idea that women are second-class
citizens. The big battles that were won in that period of civil
war and strife you cannot reverse." [40]

A week later, on April 12, 1989, he locked the door of his
apartment, poured the equivalent of 150 capsules of Phenobar-
bital into a glass of scotch, drank the mixture, got into bed with
his clothes on, and went to sleep for the last time. He was thinking about the sixties during his last days. Shortly before committing suicide, he had asked, "Can it happen again?" And he
answered "No way. It is never going to happen again." [41] He was
fifty-two.

RENNIE DAVIS had been one of the most talented and effective leaders of the antiwar movement, and one of the most sane,

at a time when many people were not; his transformation during the seventies was therefore the most upsetting and disheartening. At first he continued working as an antiwar organizer of big national mobilizations, in May 1970 and again in May 1971, a demonstration whose announced goal was to "stop the government"—it ended with some 13,000 demonstrators arrested. He demonstrated at the 1972 Republican National Convention in Miami, where Nixon was renominated, and again at the protests against Nixon's second inauguration in January 1973. That month, when the United States signed the peace treaty ending our part in the war, Rennie went to Paris for the signing.

The next chapter of his life we know mainly from Tom Hayden, who had been his best friend and closest comrade. Rennie was given a free plane ticket to India by a former roommate, a follower of an obscure Indian guru, the fifteen-year-old Guru Maharaj Ji (not to be confused with the Beatles' guru, Maharishi Mahesh Yogi). When Rennie came back, he told Tom, "I know you'll think this is crazy, that I've gone out of my mind." He described a classic conversion experience—a "total and ecstatic" moment in which he lost his identity and felt helpless. He declared he was going to devote his life to converting people to the guru and the guru's Divine Light Mission, starting with organizing a giant event at the Houston Astrodome. He told Tom that he would get John Lennon and Bob Dylan to headline, that Walter Cronkite would cover it, and that a hundred thousand converts would participate. Tom later wrote that, seeing this transformation of his best friend, "I thought I was going to be ill."[42]

1974 brought a rift to the organization when Guru Maharaj Ji, then sixteen years old, married a twenty-five-year-old flight attendant. According to *People* magazine, the guru's mother disowned him on the grounds that he drank alcohol, ate meat, and visited nightclubs. She took control of the organization and fired the mahatmas who didn't support her side of the split.[43]

Rennie left the guru's operation and, according to his website, in the 1980s became "the managing partner for a consulting company with an exclusive clientele of board members and officers of Fortune 500 companies and wealthy private families." In the 1990s he spent four years on "sabbatical," spending time in the desert. There, he later told interviewers, he arrived at a profound insight into the human condition: "the cause of misery" is not "things outside 'myself' "; rather "fear is within ourself. . . . It all comes from within." He regarded this as "a new vision as earth-shattering and radical a quantum shift in collective consciousness as when the earth went from flat to round."[44]

To spread his new vision, he became a venture capitalist and self-awareness lecturer. As of 2005 he has a company he calls "Ventures for Humanity," a limited partnership based in Las Vegas whose goal is "to commercialize breakthrough technologies." According to the company website, their projects include a "Clean Air Tool" that will allow all of humanity to "return the air to the pristine condition of a pre-industrial age"; and "Future Glass," a "breakthrough discovery" to create "thin television display screens . . . the size of a tall glass building."[45]

JERRY RUBIN had been famous for coining the slogan "Don't trust anyone over thirty." He faced an inevitable personal crisis after he turned thirty in 1968. In the middle of the Chicago trial he published a book titled *Do It!*—the back cover described it as "The Communist Manifesto of our era . . . a Declaration of War between the generations—calling on the kids to leave their homes, burn down their schools and create a new society upon the ashes of the old." [46] Despite the overheated rhetoric, by 1972 he was arguing for "working within the system" to elect McGovern, which earned him the ridicule of a younger generation of post-Yippie activists.

He had a brilliant insight as the era came to an end: he saw that a lot of youth rebels of the sixties would become successful entrepreneurs in the seventies, that elements of the counterculture would soon permeate mainstream culture, especially in advertising and media. He decided to lead the way with a high-profile transformation from Yippie to yuppie, cutting his hair, putting on a business suit, and going to work on Wall Street. He set up "networking salons" where aspiring young entrepreneurs paid big money to meet one another at trendy clubs in Manhattan. He did his best to be upbeat and optimistic, but the media were brutal about his transformation, regularly ridiculing him.

He described his transformation in a 1976 book, *Growing (Up) at 37*: "We activists in the 1960s eventually lost touch with ourselves. . . . In the consciousness movement of the '70s, I have a new vision: a loving person without expectations, who lives in his senses and in the moment." [47] During the eighties he did a college lecture tour with Abbie Hoffman titled "Yippie versus Yuppie" where they argued in public, Abbie accusing him of having sold out—the tour was immensely successful. He focused his entrepreneurial energies on health foods and in 1991 moved to Los Angeles to become a marketer for a Texas company selling a drink called "Wow."

He died on November 28, 1994, after being hit by a car while jaywalking across Wilshire Boulevard near UCLA in West Los Angeles. He was fifty-six.[48] Tom Hayden argues that Jerry was misunderstood after the trial: "He never became a right-winger," Hayden told me; "an entrepreneur, a venture capitalist, yes; a Republican, no."

DAVE DELLINGER remained a full-time antiwar activist after the trial. He helped plan demonstrations at the Democratic National Convention in Miami in 1972, where George McGovern was nominated. While Jerry Rubin and Abbie Hoffman supported McGovern, Dellinger opposed him for betraying his principles in order to win the nomination—for opposing gay rights and a guaranteed minimum income for poor people.[49]

Dellinger wrote several books after the trial, including the 1996 memoir *From Yale to Jail: The Life Story of a Moral Dissenter*. He returned to the question of whether he regretted opposing Humphrey in 1968, in view of all the damage Nixon had done to the country. Dellinger stood fast with his original argument that Humphrey's record had made it impossible to support him.

In 1992 he participated with a dozen other people in a "People's Fast for Justice and Peace in the Americas," and fasted for forty-two days. The fast coincided with Columbus Day, and Dellinger often spoke about Columbus's abuse of the Arawak. Mostly he concentrated on the opportunities the United States faced—after the collapse of the Soviet Union—to end the evils of militarism, racism, and capitalism.[50]

During the 1996 Democratic convention Dellinger went to Chicago to speak at a "Stop the Drug War" rally in Grant

Park. When the United States bombed Yugoslavia, he sat-in in the office of his congressman, Bernie Sanders, in opposition to Sanders's support of the decision. When Dellinger was eighty-three, he was arrested demonstrating against a nuclear reactor. When he was eighty-five, he got up at 3 A.M. and hitchhiked to Quebec City to demonstrate against the North American Free Trade Agreement. He died in 2004 in Vermont at age eighty-eight.[51]

BOBBY SEALE had been arrested in May 1969—three months before he was indicted as part of the Chicago conspiracy—and charged with murder in Connecticut, accused along with seven other Panthers of the torture-killing in New Haven of a New York Black Panther Party member believed to be a police informant. Seale was indicted by the New Haven grand jury in August on charges of ordering the execution. At the time the Chicago conspiracy trial began, he was being held in jail in San Francisco on the Connecticut charges.

The New Haven trial was the center of Seale's life in 1970. On January 1, 1970, two months after Seale's case was severed from the rest of the Chicago Conspiracy, California's governor, Ronald Reagan, ordered his extradition to New Haven for trial on the murder charges. The New Haven trial of the Panthers became a national political issue—a May 1 rally there attracted more than 10,000 people, mostly students. Yale students went on strike, and one of their demands was freedom for Seale and the other Panthers on trial. In the trial, two New Haven Panthers pled guilty to second-degree murder charges and a third was convicted of conspiracy, but none would implicate Seale, and the charges against him were eventually dropped.[52]

The New Haven charges were part of a campaign to destroy the Black Panther Party, initiated by FBI director J. Edgar Hoover, who had declared in June 1969 that "the Black Panther Party, without question, represents the greatest threat to internal security of the country." The 1970 Annual Report of the FBI declared that the Panthers were the nation's "most dangerous and violence-prone of all extremist groups."[53] In 1970, Party attorney Charles Garry claimed that twenty-eight Panthers had been killed by the police, while many others were in jail, and some, like Eldridge Cleaver, had gone into exile to avoid prison. (Edward Jay Epstein showed in a 1971 article that in fact "only" ten Panthers had been killed by the police.)[54]

In 1973 Seale ran for mayor of Oakland, winning 40 percent of the vote. The Party went into decline as its leaders split; first Seale broke with Eldridge Cleaver—Seale, along with co-founder Huey Newton, favored community programs, while Cleaver, in exile in Algeria, called for revolution. Then Huey Newton fled to Cuba in 1974 to avoid drug charges. Seale resigned as chairman of the Party that year.[55] In 1978 he published an autobiography, *A Lonely Rage*, describing his childhood experiences. (An earlier autobiography had been published in 1970: *Seize the Time.*)

Today Bobby Seale's website (www.BobbySeale.com) offers videos and lectures on the history and legacy of the Black Panther Party as well as a barbecue cookbook.

JOHN FROINES today is a distinguished chemist who served as Occupational Safety and Health Administration Director of Toxic Substances during the Carter Administration. In 1981 he joined the UCLA faculty as a professor of environmental health sciences. Today he is Director of the UCLA Center for

Occupational and Environmental Health, and Director of the UCLA-Mexico/Latin America Training and Research Program. The program has trained hundreds of Mexican students, professionals, and government officials.

LEE WEINER worked for years in Washington as a specialist in direct-mail for nonprofit organizations and political candidates. In the mid-nineties he became director of special projects for the Anti-Defamation League in New York City.

LEONARD WEINGLASS went on to a distinguished career as one of America's leading radical lawyers. He represented Mumia abu Jamal, challenging Mumia's death sentence until, in 2001, he was dismissed from the defense team. He got Kathy Boudin out of jail in 2003 after she had served twenty-two years for participating in the murder of two police officers as part of a black radical group's armored-car holdup that went wrong.

WILLIAM KUNSTLER remained a flamboyant and high-profile attorney for the unpopular. He defended leaders of the American Indian Movement, flag-burner Joey Johnson, and mobster John Gotti, along with the Muslim extremist who shot and killed Rabbi Meir Kahane. In 1994 he published a memoir, *My Life as a Radical Lawyer.* He died at age seventy-six in September 1995.

TOM HAYDEN after the trial intensified his antiwar work before the 1972 election, organizing the Indochina Peace Campaign, whose strategy was to shun the more marginal elements of the Left and work in the mainstream. With Jane Fonda, Holly Near, and others, he toured the country, speaking several times a day and visiting ninety cities. The campaign supported McGovern for president. He and Jane Fonda married and had a baby.

When the war finally ended, in 1975, Hayden decided to enter electoral politics and challenge the incumbent Democratic senator, John Tunney, in the California primary in 1976. The idea was to build a statewide grassroots political organization that would extend the energies of the antiwar movement into new political areas after the war. With the help of many others, his campaign developed a program that proposed challenging "Government of the Corporations" in the name of "Government of the People." Tunney, a mainstream Democrat, led in the initial polls, 55 to 15 percent. On election day Tunney got 54 percent, but Hayden had increased his support to 37 percent, which, he later wrote, "felt like a victory." [56]

With Democrats in both the White House (Jimmy Carter) and the state house in Sacramento (Jerry Brown), Tom's new organization, the Campaign for Economic Democracy, elected local candidates throughout the state, won rent-control legislation, and fought nuclear power. Working from a base in Santa Monica, Hayden won election to the California assembly in 1992 and the state senate in 1992, winning seven elections and serving a total of eighteen years, always as a Democrat. He fought for immigrants working in sweatshops, students facing higher tuition, against the tobacco industry, for the environment. The *Sacramento Bee* called him "the conscience of the Senate." [57] He wrote several books, including a wonderful memoir, *Reunion*.

The massive antiglobalization demonstrations in the streets of Seattle in 1999 convinced Hayden that a new generation had set new standards for commitment and militancy. After being termed out of office in the state legislature in 1999, he narrowly lost a campaign for Los Angeles city council, and he began teaching at Occidental College. In 2005, as the war in Iraq came more and more to resemble the war in Vietnam, Tom was organizing a campaign around "An exit strategy for Iraq now." [58]

Chronology

This chronology is abridged from "Chicago '68: A Chronology" by Dean Blobaum, published at http://www.geocities .com/dblobaum/, and is used with his permission.

1967

October 21–22: A demonstration at the Pentagon organized by the National Mobilization to End the War in Vietnam ("the Mobe") draws about 100,000. Afterward, the Mobe begins to talk about organizing antiwar protests during the 1968 Democratic National Convention, where President Johnson is expected to be nominated for a second term.

November 30: Senator Eugene McCarthy officially enters the race for the Democratic presidential nomination, challenging President Johnson with an antiwar platform.

December 31: Activists partying at Abbie Hoffman's New York loft resolve to hold a Festival of Life during the Democrats' "Convention of Death." Paul Krassner christens the group "Yippies."

1968

January 30: The Tet Offensive begins in South Vietnam; Vietcong and North Vietnamese troops strike at targets across South Vietnam, reaching even the grounds of the U.S. Embassy in Saigon. The turning point in public support for the war.

February 1: Richard Nixon enters the race for the Republican nomination for president.

March 12: Eugene McCarthy comes close to defeating Johnson in the New Hampshire primary, demonstrating the unpopularity of the president and the war.

March 16: Senator Robert Kennedy reverses his earlier decision and announces his candidacy.

March 22–23: A Mobe conference in Lake Villa, Illinois, brings together Mobe, Students for a Democratic Society (SDS), and Yippie activists to plan the Convention demonstrations.

March 31: Lyndon Johnson declares he will not run for reelection.

April 4: Reverend Martin Luther King Jr. is assassinated in Memphis, Tennessee. Riots break out in more than one hun-

dred cities. On the west side of Chicago, nine blacks are killed
and twenty city blocks are burned.

April 11: President Johnson signs the Civil Rights Act of 1968.
While primarily addressing open housing, the act also includes
a new federal antiriot law, making it a crime to cross state lines
with the intent to incite a riot.

April 15: Chicago Mayor Richard J. Daley publicly criticizes
Superintendent of Police James Conlisk's cautious handling of
the riots that followed King's assassination. He said he was giv-
ing the police specific instructions "to shoot to kill any arsonist
and to shoot to maim or cripple anyone looting."

April 23: At Columbia University in New York, students opposed to defense contracts and a new gymnasium to be built on
Harlem park land occupy several campus buildings. They are
routed by city police a week later: 150 injuries, 700 arrests.

April 27: Vice President Hubert H. Humphrey announces his
candidacy for the Democratic presidential nomination.

May 6–30: Student demonstrations in France lead to a general
strike throughout the country. Ten million workers strike,
10,000 battle police in Paris.

May 10: Peace talks open in Paris with Averell Harriman
representing the United States and Xan Thuy representing North Vietnam. Talks soon deadlock over the North
Vietnamese demand for an end to all U.S. bombing of North

Vietnam. More than 2,000 American soldiers die in combat in May, the highest monthly loss of the war.

May 14: J. Edgar Hoover, director of the FBI, sends a memorandum to all FBI field offices initiating a counterintelligence program (COINTELPRO) to disrupt new left groups.

June 5: Senator Robert Kennedy is assassinated in Los Angeles moments after declaring victory in the California Democratic presidential primary.

July 15: The Yippies apply for permits to camp in Lincoln Park (about two miles north of the Chicago Loop) and to rally at Soldier Field (on the lakefront south of the Loop).

July 29: The Mobe applies for permits to march to and rally at the International Amphitheatre (site of the Democratic Convention and about five miles southwest of the Loop) and to march to and rally in Grant Park (just east of the Loop). All permits are denied, except one allowing the use of the Grant Park bandshell for a rally.

August 8: At the Republican National Convention in Miami Beach, Florida, Richard M. Nixon wins the party's nomination for president. At the same time, not far away in the black neighborhoods of Miami, riots result in four deaths and hundreds of arrests.

August 10: Senator George S. McGovern announces his candidacy for the Democratic presidential nomination.

August 21: Soviet tanks and troops roll into Czechoslovakia to crush the "Prague Spring" reform movement.

Convention Week

August 23, Friday: At the Civic Center plaza (located in the Loop and now known as the Daley Center) the Yippies nominate their presidential contender—Pigasus the pig. Seven Yippies and the pig are arrested.

Almost 6,000 National Guardsman are mobilized and practice riot-control drills. Special police platoons do the same.

August 24, Saturday: The Mobe's marshal-training sessions continue in Lincoln Park. Karate, snake dancing, and crowd protection techniques are practiced. Women Strike for Peace holds a women-only picket at the Hilton Hotel, where many delegates are staying. At the 11 P.M. curfew, poet Allen Ginsberg, chanting, and musician Ed Sanders lead people out of the park.

August 25, Sunday: The Mobe's "Meet the Delegates" march gathers about 800 protesters in Grant Park across from the Hilton Hotel. The Festival of Life, in Lincoln Park, opens with music; five thousand hear the MC-5 and local bands play. Police refuse to allow a flatbed truck to be brought in as a stage. A fracas breaks out in which several are arrested and others are clubbed. Police reinforcements arrive.

At the 11 P.M. curfew, most of the crowd, now numbering around 2,000, leave the park ahead of a police sweep. The police line then moves into the crowd, pushing it into the street. Many are clubbed, reporters and photographers included. The crowd disperses into the Old Town area, where the battles continue.

August 26, Monday: In the early morning, Tom Hayden is among those arrested. One thousand protesters march toward police headquarters at Eleventh and State. Dozens of officers surround the building. The march turns north to Grand Park, swarming the General Logan statue. Police react by clearing the hill and the statue.

At the Amphitheatre, Mayor Daley formally opens the 1968 Democratic National Convention.

As the curfew approaches, some in Lincoln Park build a barricade against the police line to the east. About 1,000 remain in the park after 11 P.M. A police car noses into the barricade and is pelted by rocks. Police move in with tear gas. Like Sunday night, street violence ensues. But it is worse. Some area residents are pulled off their porches and clubbed. More reporters are attacked this night than at any other time during the week.

August 27, Tuesday: About 7 P.M., Black Panther Party Chairman Bobby Seale speaks in Lincoln Park. He urges people to defend themselves by any means necessary if attacked by the police.

An "Unbirthday Party for LBJ" convenes at the Chicago Coliseum. Performers and speakers include Ed Sanders, Abbie Hoffman, David Dellinger, Terry Southern, Jean Genet, William Burroughs, Dick Gregory, Allen Ginsberg, Phil Ochs, and Rennie Davis. Two thousand later march from the Coliseum to Grant Park.

In Lincoln Park, about two thousand protestors remain in the park past curfew. Again, tear gas and club-swinging police clear the park.

At Grant Park, in front of the Hilton, where the television cameras are, some 4,000 demonstrators rally to speeches by Julian Bond, Rennie Davis, and Tom Hayden. The rally is peaceful. At 3 A.M. the National Guard relieve the police. The crowd is allowed to stay in Grant Park all night.

August 28, Wednesday: Between 10,000 and 15,000 people gather at the old Grant Park bandshell for the Mobe's antiwar rally. Dellinger, Gregory, Ginsberg, Norman Mailer, Jerry Rubin, Carl Oglesby, Hayden, and many others speak. Six hundred police surround the rally on all sides.

At the convention inside the Amphitheatre, the peace plank proposed for the Democratic party platform is voted down.

At the bandshell rally, news of the defeat of the peace plank is heard on radios. A young man climbs the flagpole near the bandshell. Police push through the crowd to arrest him. A line of Mobe marshals is formed between the police and the crowd. Police charge the marshal line. Rennie Davis is beaten unconscious.

At rally's end, Dellinger announces a march to the Amphitheatre. Six thousand join the march line, but the police refuse to allow it to move. Thousands surge onto Michigan Avenue. The police try to clear the streets: demonstrators and bystanders are clubbed, beaten, Maced, and arrested. Some fight back and the attack escalates. The melee lasts about seventeen minutes and is filmed by the TV crews positioned at the Hilton. While this is probably not the most violent episode of Convention Week—the Lincoln Park and Old Town brawls were more vicious—it draws the most attention from the mass media.

Inside the Amphitheatre, presidential nominations are under way. Senator Abraham Ribicoff, in his speech nominating George McGovern, denounces the "Gestapo tactics on the streets of Chicago." Mayor Daley's shouted reaction was on-camera, but off-mike. Lip-readers saw him yelling "Fuck you, you Jew son-of-a-bitch, you lousy mother-fucker, go home." Hubert H. Humphrey wins the party's nomination on the first ballot.

Five hundred antiwar delegates march from the Amphitheatre to the Hilton; many join the 4,000 protestors in Grant Park. Again, protestors are allowed to stay in the park all night.

August 29, Thursday: Senator Eugene McCarthy addresses about 5,000 gathered in Grant Park. Several attempts are made to march to the Amphitheatre. A group of delegates try to lead a march but are turned back with tear gas.

Near midnight, the 1968 Democratic National Convention is adjourned. The arrest count for Convention Week disturbances stands at 668. An undetermined number of demonstrators have sustained injuries, with hospitals reporting that they have treated 111 demonstrators. The on-the-street medical teams from the Medical Committee for Human Rights estimate that their medics have treated more than 1,000 demonstrators at the scene. The police department reports that 192 officers were injured, with forty-nine officers seeking hospital treatment.

August 30, Friday: During Convention Week, 308 Americans have been killed and 1,144 more injured in the war in Vietnam.

September 9: In a press conference, Mayor Daley declares, "The policeman isn't there to create disorder, the policeman is there to preserve disorder."

November 5: Nixon is elected, defeating Humphrey by about 600,000 votes. George Wallace receives about 13 percent of the vote nationwide and wins five Southern states.

December 1: Public release of *Rights in Conflict*, commonly called the Walker Report. The National Commission on the Causes and Prevention of Violence, charged with studying the Convention Week disturbances, review more than 20,000 pages of statements from 3,437 eyewitnesses and participants, 180 hours of film, and more than 12,000 still photographs. The Walker Report concludes that the events of Chicago '68 were a "police riot."

1969

January 20: Nixon is inaugurated as president.

March 20: Rennie Davis, David Dellinger, John Froines, Tom Hayden, Abbie Hoffman, Jerry Rubin, Bobby Seale, and Lee Weiner are indicted on federal charges of conspiring to cross state lines "with the intent to incite, organize, promote, encourage, participate in, and carry out a riot." Six defendants—Dellinger, Hayden, Davis, Hoffman, Rubin, and Seale—are also individually charged with crossing state lines with the intent to incite a riot. Each of the two charges carries a five-year sentence; each defendant thus faces a ten-year prison term. The indictment charges that Froines and Weiner, in addition to the conspiracy charge, "did teach and demonstrate to other persons the use, application and making of an incendiary device."

The same federal grand jury that returned these criminal indictments also charged eight Chicago policemen with civil rights violations for assaulting demonstrators and news reporters. None of the policemen were convicted. (Forty-one officers of the Chicago Police Department were disciplined after internal investigations, and two resigned, for infractions such as removing their badges and nameplates while on duty during Convention Week.)

June 8: Gradual withdrawal of U.S. forces from Vietnam begins as Nixon announces that about 25,000 troops will be withdrawn.

September 24: The Chicago Eight conspiracy trial begins in the courtroom of Judge Julius Hoffman.

October 8–11: The Weatherman faction of SDS holds its National Actions—the Days of Rage—in Chicago. Turnout is tiny. Pipe-wielding Weathermen race through the streets, attacking police, windows, and cars.

October 15: An estimated two million people in cities across the country participate in the first Moratorium Day against the war.

October 29: Bobby Seale is bound and gagged in the court-room after repeatedly asserting his right to an attorney of his own choosing or to defend himself.

November 5: A mistrial is declared in the case of Bobby Seale and a new, separate trial is ordered. The Chicago Eight become the Chicago Seven. Seale is sentenced to four years for con-tempt of court; the sentence is later reversed. Seale is never convicted of any Convention Week charges.

November 15: A Mobe-organized march draws about 500,000 people to Washington, D.C.; 150,000 attend a march in San Francisco.

December 4: In an early-morning raid, Chicago police fire nearly one hundred shots into a West Side apartment. Illinois Black Panther Party Chairman Fred Hampton and Party mem-ber Mark Clark are killed.

1970

February 18: The Chicago Seven conspiracy trial ends. All defendants are acquitted on conspiracy charges. Froines and Weiner are acquitted on all charges. Davis, Dellinger, Hayden, Hoffman, and Rubin are each convicted of crossing state lines to incite violence; each is sentenced to five years in prison and fined $5,000. All the defendants, plus their lawyers

William Kunstler and Leonard Weinglass, are cited for contempt of court, with sentences ranging from two-and-a-half months to four years. Defendants are freed on bail pending an appeal.

April 30: American troops cross over the border into Cambodia to destroy enemy camps and supplies. Student strikes shut down hundreds of college campuses over the next few days.

May 4: Four students are killed and nine injured by National Guard troops during protests at Kent State University in Ohio. In the aftermath, demonstrations spread to more than 1,000 campuses, and 100,000 rally in Washington, D.C.

May 15: At Jackson State College in Mississippi, two students are killed and twelve are injured when city police and highway patrolmen fire on a dormitory building.

1972

February 8: An appeal of the convictions of Dellinger, Hayden, Davis, Hoffman, and Rubin on the individual charges of crossing state lines with the intent to incite a riot is heard by the Seventh Circuit Court of Appeals.

February 9: An appeal of the contempt sentences of the Chicago Seven and their attorneys is heard by the Seventh Circuit Court of Appeals. In a separate proceeding an appeal of the contempt sentences of Bobby Seale is also argued.

May 11: Ruling by the Seventh Circuit Court of Appeals voids a few of the contempt citations of the Chicago Seven and their attorneys, but remands the rest for retrial by a judge other than Julius Hoffman. The court also reverses the contempt sentences for Seale. (The government decides not to proceed with a contempt trial for Seale, but to go to trial on the contempt charges against the Chicago Seven and attorneys Kunstler and Weinglass.)

June 17: Five men are arrested in a break-in at the Democratic National Committee offices in Washington's Watergate complex.

November 1: Ruling by the Seventh Circuit Court of Appeals on the convictions of Dellinger, Hayden, Davis, Hoffman, and Rubin for crossing state lines with the intent to incite a riot. Citing judicial error, the convictions are reversed and a new trial is ordered. The court adds "that the demeanor of the judge and the prosecutors would require reversal if the other errors did not."

November 7: Nixon is reelected to a second term as president, defeating George McGovern.

1973

January 4: The U.S. Attorney's Office announces that it will not seek a new trial on the individual counts of Dellinger, Hayden, Davis, Hoffman, and Rubin.

January 27: U.S. War in Vietnam ends with signing of the Paris Peace Agreement.

October 29: Trial on the contempt citations of the Chicago Seven and their attorneys before Judge Edward T. Gignoux, a U.S. district court judge from Maine. The court rules that 146 of Judge Hoffman's citations were not valid. Hayden, Davis, Froines, Weiner, and Weinglass are cleared of all contempt charges. Rubin, Hoffman, and Kunstler are found guilty of two contempts each. Dellinger is found guilty of seven contempts. However, in consideration of "judicial error, judicial or prosecutorial misconduct, and judicial or prosecutorial provocation," no sentences are imposed.

1974

July 27–30: The House Judiciary Committee votes three articles of impeachment against President Nixon in connection with the Watergate burglary.

August 9: Facing possible impeachment and eroding public support, Nixon resigns.

1975

April 30: The last American personnel in Vietnam leave via helicopter from the roof of the U.S. embassy as Saigon becomes Ho Chi Minh City.

Trial Transcript

I.

Opening Statements

September 26, 1969

The eight defendants were charged with a conspiracy to travel interstate "with the intent to incite, organize, promote, encourage, participate in, and carry out a riot." Rennie Davis, Dave Dellinger, Tom Hayden, Abbie Hoffman, Jerry Rubin, and Bobby Seale faced one additional charge of inciting violence. Each of the charges, conspiracy and incitement, carried a five-year sentence; each defendant thus faced a ten-year prison term. John Froines and Lee Weiner were charged not with incitement, but with teaching others how to make incendiary devices.

FOR THE GOVERNMENT:

Richard G. Schultz was the assistant U.S. attorney. During the convention demonstrations he had served as a liaison between federal authorities and the Chicago police.

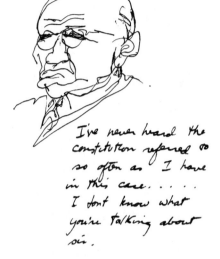

I've never heard the
constitution referred to
so often as I have
in this case. . . . .
I don't know what
you're talking about
sir.

Judge Julius Hoffman

RICHARD SCHULTZ: The Government, ladies and gentlemen of the jury, will prove in this case, the case which you will witness as jurors, an overall plan of the eight defendants in this case which was to encourage numerous people to come to the city of Chicago, people who planned legitimate protest during the Democratic National Convention which was held in Chicago in August of 1968, from August 26 through August 29, 1968. They planned to bring these people in to Chicago to protest, legitimately protest, as I said, creating a situation in this city where these people would come to Chicago, would riot. The defendants, in perpetrating this offense, they, the defendants, crossed state lines themselves, at least six of them, with intent to incite this riot.

Richard Schultz, assistant U.S. attorney

The jury was excused from the courtroom.

JUDGE HOFFMAN: This will be but a minute, Mr. Marshal. Who is the last defendant you named?

RICHARD SCHULTZ: Mr. Hayden.

JUDGE HOFFMAN: Hayden. Who was the one before?

RICHARD SCHULTZ: Davis, and prior to that was Dellinger.

JUDGE HOFFMAN: The one that shook his fist in the direction of the jury?

TOM HAYDEN: That is my customary greeting, your Honor.

JUDGE HOFFMAN: It may be your customary greeting but we do not allow shaking of fists in this courtroom. I made that clear.

Tom Hayden

TOM HAYDEN: It implied no disrespect for the jury; it is my customary greeting.

JUDGE HOFFMAN: Regardless of what it implies, sir, there will be no fist shaking and I caution you not to repeat it.

The jury returned and Richard Schultz continued with his opening statement.

RICHARD SCHULTZ: The defendants Dellinger, Davis, and Hayden joined with five other defendants who are charged in this case in their venture to succeed in their plans to create the riots in Chicago during the time the Democratic National Convention was convened here.

Two of these defendants, the defendant Abbie Hoffman who sits—who is just standing for you, ladies and gentlemen.

JUDGE HOFFMAN: The jury is directed to disregard the kiss thrown by the defendant Hoffman and the defendant is directed not to do that sort of thing again.

RICHARD SCHULTZ: Ladies and gentlemen of the jury, the Government will prove that each of these eight men assumed specific roles in it and they united and that the eight conspired together to encourage people to riot during the convention. We will prove that the plans to incite the riot were basically in three steps. The first step was to use the unpopularity of the war in Vietnam as a method to urge people to come to Chicago during that convention for purposes of protest.

The second step was to incite these people who came to Chicago, against the police department, the city officials, the National Guard and the military, and against the convention itself, so that these people would physically resist and defy the orders of the police and the military.

The third step was to create a situation where the demonstrators who had come to Chicago and would meet and would confront the police in the streets of Chicago so that at this confrontation a riot would occur.

In sum, then, ladies and gentlemen, the Government will prove that the eight defendants charged here conspired together to use interstate commerce and the facilities of interstate commerce to incite and to further a riot in Chicago.

FOR THE DEFENSE:

William Kunstler was a dramatic courtroom figure who had argued many civil rights cases in the South; he had represented Martin Luther King, Black Panthers Stokely Carmichael and H. Rap Brown, and Malcolm X.

WILLIAM KUNSTLER: Now the Government has given you its table of contents. I will present to you in general what the Defense hopes to show is the true book. We hope to prove before you that the evidence submitted by the defendants will show that this prosecution which you are hearing is the result of two motives on the part of the Government—

RICHARD SCHULTZ: Objection as to any motives of the prosecution, if the Court please.

WILLIAM KUNSTLER: Your Honor, it is a proper defense to show motive.

JUDGE HOFFMAN: I sustain the objection. You may speak to the guilt or innocence of your clients, not to the motive of the Government.

WILLIAM KUNSTLER: The evidence will show as far as the defendants are concerned that they, like many other citizens of

William Kunstler, defense attorney

the United States, numbering in the many thousands, came to Chicago in the summer of 1968 to protest in the finest American tradition outside and in the vicinity of the convention, the national convention of the party in power. They came to protest the continuation of a war in South Vietnam which was then and had been for many years past within the jurisdiction of the Democratic Party at that time.

The possibility of influencing delegates to that national convention to take an affirmative strong stand against a continuation of this bloody and unjustified war, as they considered it to be along with millions of persons, was one of the prime purposes of their coming to Chicago.

At the same time as they were making plans to stage this

demonstration and seeking every legal means in which to do so, at the same time as all of this was going on, the evidence will show that there were forces in this city and in the national government who were absolutely determined to prevent this type of protest, who had reached a conclusion that such a protest had to be stopped by the—the same phrase used by Mr. Schultz—by all means necessary, including the physical violence perpetrated on demonstrators. These plans were gathering in Washington and they were gathering here in this city, and long before a single demonstrator had set foot in the city of Chicago in the summer of 1968, the determination had been made that these demonstrations would be diffused, they would be dissipated, they would essentially be destroyed as effective demonstrations against primarily the continuation of the war in South Vietnam.

We will demonstrate that free speech died here in the streets under those clubs and that the bodies of these demonstrators were the sacrifices to its death.

The Defense will show that the real conspiracy in this case is the conspiracy to curtail and prevent the demonstrations against the war in Vietnam and related issues that these defendants and other people, thousands, who came here were determined to present to the delegates of a political party and the party in power meeting in Chicago; that the real conspiracy was against these defendants. But we are going to show that the real conspiracy is not against these defendants as individuals because they are unimportant as individuals: the real attempt was—the real attack was on the rights of everybody, all of us American citizens, all, to protest under the First Amendment to the Constitution, to protest against a war that was brutalizing us all.

Dissent died here for a moment during that Democratic National Convention. What happens in this case may determine whether it is moribund.

Leonard Weinglass was a younger, less well known, and less flamboyant figure than Kunstler.

LEONARD WEINGLASS: The people who were in charge of granting to these young people the right which they have as citizens to congregate, and meet, and we contend even sleep in our public parks, which are publicly owned property held in trust for the public by the public officials, were reasonable demands which the city could have met if the persons responsible for that

Leonard Weinglass, defense attorney

decision would not have been persons who were so fearful and so misunderstood the young in this country that they could not meet and talk to them in a reasonable, rational way.

I might say at to you at the outset I do not ask you to accept, or like, or understand, or agree with any of the speeches which my clients might have given.

Thomas Foran was a U.S. attorney and the main prosecutor. Earlier, Chicago Mayor Richard Daley had appointed him to a City Hall position. Before the convention, Rennie Davis had asked him to help the demonstrators obtain permits from the city. During the convention protests, he served as a liaison between federal authorities and the Chicago police.

THOMAS FORAN: Your Honor, once again, counsel continues to argue the case. It is improper.

JUDGE HOFFMAN: I sustain the objection. Do I make myself clear to you?

LEONARD WEINGLASS: I am having a little difficulty applying your Honor's ruling to my opening statement.

JUDGE HOFFMAN: If you persist, I will have to deprive you of the right to proceed further.

LEONARD WEINGLASS: [*to the jury*] We want to bring before you a full, a clear picture of what happened. While the Government is presenting its case, [we] will be making certain objections.

JUDGE HOFFMAN: I have repeatedly cautioned you. I caution you again, Mr. Weinglass. I think you understand me. You persist in arguing and telling the jury what you propose to do in respect to objections.

Thomas Foran, chief U.S. attorney

LEONARD WEINGLASS: Yes, I thought that was the purpose of an opening statement.

JUDGE HOFFMAN: That is not the function of an opening statement. I have cautioned you time and time again. I caution you once more.

LEONARD WEINGLASS: I thought that was the purpose of an opening statement. Thank you, your Honor.

JUDGE HOFFMAN: Don't thank me. I didn't do it as a favor to you. I am cautioning you not to persist in it.

LEONARD WEINGLASS: My last comment to you, ladies and gentlemen of the jury, is that we of the Defense do consider you in this courtroom to be the highest authority, and we will—

Weinglass was about to advocate the radical doctrine of "jury nullification," holding that the jury could judge not only the defendants but also the law.

JUDGE HOFFMAN: Ladies and gentlemen of the jury—

THOMAS FORAN: This is argument.

JUDGE HOFFMAN: I will sustain the objection.

The jury was excused from the courtroom.

JUDGE HOFFMAN: Mr. Weinglass, I think your persistency in disregarding the direction of the Court and the law in the face of repeated admonitions is contumacious conduct, and I so find it on the record.

The jury returned.

JUDGE HOFFMAN: Does any other Defense lawyer wish to make an opening statement? Just a minute, sir, who is your lawyer?

BOBBY SEALE: Charles R. Garry.

The jury was excused.

Bobby Seale and Judge Hoffman

Charles R. Garry was indeed Bobby Seale's lawyer, but two weeks before the trial began, he had had emergency gallbladder surgery and had requested a six-week postponement in the trial. Even though postponements are granted all the time for all sorts of reasons, Judge Hoffman had refused to grant this one, and he insisted that William Kunstler represent Bobby Seale—even though Bobby Seale had a clear constitutional right to be represented by the counsel of his choice. Seale's insistence on this right provided the central drama of the first part of the trial.

JUDGE HOFFMAN: Mr. Kunstler, do you represent Mr. Seale?

WILLIAM KUNSTLER: No, your Honor, as far as Mr. Seale has indicated to me, that because of the absence of Charles R. Garry—

JUDGE HOFFMAN: I will permit you to make another opening statement on behalf of Mr. Seale if you like. I will not permit a party to a case to—

WILLIAM KUNSTLER: Your Honor, I cannot compromise Mr. Seale's position—

JUDGE HOFFMAN: I don't ask you to compromise it, sir, but I will not permit him to address the jury with his very competent lawyer seated there.

WILLIAM KUNSTLER: If I were to make an opening statement, I would compromise his position that he has not his full counsel here.

JUDGE HOFFMAN: Mr. Seale, you are not to make an opening statement. I so order you. You are not permitted to in the circumstances of this case.

II.

The Government's Case

JUDGE HOFFMAN: Will you call your first witness?

Government Witness Raymond Simon, corporation counsel for the City of Chicago

Simon was the city's top attorney; Abbie Hoffman and Jerry Rubin had met with him on August 8, two weeks before the convention, requesting a permit for the demonstrators to use Lincoln Park. When the city turned them down, the National Mobilization Committee, led by Rennie Davis, Tom Hayden, and others, had filed a lawsuit seeking a permit. Simon was asked about a meeting in the chambers of Judge Lynch.

THOMAS FORAN: What did Mr. Davis say?

RAYMOND SIMON: He said, "If the city doesn't give us the park, there will be tens of thousands of people without a place to stay, and they will go into the parks, and the police will drive them out, and they will run through the streets of the city, and there'll be disorder, and conflict, and problems, and the police will fight back, and there will be tear gas, and Mace, and billy clubs."

Q: Did [Judge Lynch] issue [an] opinion the next day?
A: Yes, he dismissed the lawsuit.

September 29, 1969

Judge Hoffman began the trial with an extraordinary move: He ordered the arrest and imprisonment of four defense attorneys who had worked on pretrial motions but did not appear in court—even though such lawyers typically do not appear for the trial. Hoffman's move led 126 lawyers to file a brief calling it "a travesty of justice," and thirteen faculty members from Harvard Law School to call on the Senate Judiciary Committee to investigate Hoffman's order; even more amazing, hundreds of lawyers from around the country showed up outside Hoffman's courtroom to demonstrate against his order.

WILLIAM KUNSTLER: Your Honor, without repeating any of the long history of the controversy with reference to the lawyers which was disposed of this morning. I am moving on behalf of all defendants for a mistrial in this case or, in the alternative, again for the disqualification of this Court [*i.e. Judge Hoffman*].

Our first ground is that your Honor illegally, unlawfully, and unconstitutionally ordered and directed the arrest of some of the pretrial lawyers in the case; that equally illegally you effectuated the imprisonment and appearance in court while in custody of these attorneys; that you refused, again we claim unconstitutionally, to set bond for these attorneys, and again, number four, equally unconstitutionally, you attempted to coerce the defendants by these arrests and imprisonment and denial of bail to waive their Sixth Amendment rights to counsel of their choice; and that you have during the course of the trial degraded, harassed, and maligned in diverse ways and fashions these and other of defendants' attorneys, and because of this you have so prejudiced this case that there can no longer be a fair and impartial trial—all we claim in violation of the Constitution and laws of the United States.

JUDGE HOFFMAN: Mr. Clerk, the motion styled "Emergency Motion" filed by the defendants over the signature of William N. Kunstler and a signature of Leonard Weinglass signed as represented by William N. Kunstler for a mistrial or, in the alternative, for the disqualification of the Court [*i.e. Judge Hoffman*], will be denied.

September 30, 1969

BOBBY SEALE: I fired all of these lawyers a long time ago. Charles Garry ain't here, and I want my legal counsel here.

THOMAS FORAN: Judge, the reason we were late this morning and then the reason for the request for the interruption was I was informed just about the time we were to come to court by the FBI that they had been informed that one of the jurors had received a letter or her family had received a letter that certainly could be of a threatening nature. It is addressed to the King family, 81 South Caroline, Crystal Lake, Illinois 60014. It is written in script, "You are being watched. The Black Panthers."

The letter had been sent to the home of one of two jurors the defense considered most open to their case: Kristi King, a young woman whose sister was in VISTA, the domestic Peace Corps. Bobby Seale and the other defendants regarded the letter as bogus and suspected it was part of a plot to get rid of a juror who seemed potentially sympathetic to the defense. In fact Kristi King had not seen the letter; her parents had turned it over to the FBI. The judge nevertheless removed her—and then, in a crucial move, he sequestered the jury, putting them under continual supervision of the marshals for the rest of the trial and requiring them to stay together in a hotel rather than go home to their families each night. Cut off completely from the outside world, the jury, the defense felt, would be more under the power of the court and the prosecution.

WILLIAM KUNSTLER: Your Honor, before the jury comes in, the Defense would move for the unsequestration of the jury. We think it is more humane.

JUDGE HOFFMAN: I will deny the motion.

Government Witness David Stahl, administrative officer to Mayor Daley of Chicago

Stahl represented the city in meetings before the convention with demonstration planners. He was asked about a meeting with Abbie Hoffman and Jerry Rubin on March 26, 1968.

DAVID STAHL: I was told by Abbie Hoffman that the Youth International Party would be holding a Festival of Life in Grant Park during the week of the Democratic National Convention; that there would be five hundred thousand young people attending this Festival of Life; that they would be entertained by rock bands and that they were going to sleep in Grant Park. Abbie Hoffman said that he was prepared to tear up the town and the convention. He said that he was willing to die in Lincoln Park. Mr. Hoffman then said that if we were smart, we the City was smart, we would give them a hundred thousand dollars and they would sponsor the Festival of Life, or; he said, better still, we would give them—give him a hundred thousand dollars and he would leave town.

Cross-Examination

LEONARD WEINGLASS: Now if my understanding is correct, all of the meetings with Abbie and Jerry occurred in City Hall, the three meetings?

THOMAS FORAN: Your Honor, I object to the constant reference to these two little—to Abbie and Jerry. Let's call the defendants by their proper names.

JUDGE HOFFMAN: I agree.

THOMAS FORAN: It is an attempt to give a diminutive attitude to men who are over thirty.

JUDGE HOFFMAN: They should not be referred to in the United States district court by their—I nearly said Christian names; I don't know whether that would be accurate or not, but not by their first names.

THOMAS FORAN: Your Honor, here we go again. Now another twenty-nine-year-old being "Rennie Baby." I object to the diminutive familiar child terms for mentally grown men.

LEONARD WEINGLASS: "Rennie Baby"?

WILLIAM KUNSTLER: Would your Honor order the jury to disregard the "Rennie Baby" remark as unfounded?

JUDGE HOFFMAN: If the United States Attorney said that, I certainly do. Crowd the "Baby" out of your minds. We are not dealing with babies here.

October 2, 1969

The jury was excused.

WILLIAM KUNSTLER: I want the record to quite clearly indicate that I do not direct Mr. Seale in any way. He is a free independent black man who does his own direction.

JUDGE HOFFMAN: Black or white, sir—and what an extraordinary statement, "an independent black man." He is a defendant in this case. He will be calling you a racist before you are through, Mr. Kunstler.

WILLIAM KUNSTLER: Your Honor, I think to call him a free independent black man will not incite his anger.

The jury returned.

Now, in all of your discussions with either Jerry Rubin, Abbie Hoffman, Dave Dellinger, Rennie Davis, or any of the people with them at any of the meetings to which you testified, did anyone ever say to you, "If we don't get the permits, we're going to do violent acts in this city"?

DAVID STAHL: Not in precisely that language, no.

Q: Well, did they do it in any language?

A: Yes. Mr. Dellinger said on Monday that permits for the use of the parks should be issued in order to minimize destruction.

Q: To minimize destruction. And did he indicate to you from whence the destruction would come?

A: It certainly wasn't coming from the Chicago Police Department.

LEONARD WEINGLASS: On the August 7 meeting with Abbie Hoffman and Jerry Rubin, did Mr. Hoffman and Mr. Rubin indicate to you that if the Yippies would be permitted to stay in the park, that everything would be OK and not violent?

DAVID STAHL: I don't recall words exactly to that effect being—
or statements exactly to that effect being made at that meeting.

Q: Was that the general tenor of their remarks, Mr. Stahl?

A: They opened the meeting by saying they wanted to avoid violence. They also followed that statement subsequently with
statements about their willingness or about Mr. Hoffman's
willingness to tear up the town and the convention and to die in
Lincoln Park.

October 3, 1969

Government Witness Mary Ellen Dahl, Chicago police officer

RICHARD SCHULTZ: Now will you relate, please, to the Court
and to the jury what you heard the Defendant [Abbie] Hoffman say?

MARY ELLEN DAHL: Yes, sir. He said, "Tomorrow we're going
to meet in Grant Park, and we're going to storm the Hilton.
We got to get there singly because if we go in groups the blank
pigs are going to stop us."

Q: You say "blank pigs." Did he say "blank pigs"?

A: No, sir.

Q: Did he use another word other than "blank"?

A: Yes, sir.

Q: Was it a four-letter word?

A: Yes, sir.

Q: What was the first letter of that four-letter word, please?

A: "F."

October 7, 1969

The jury was excused.

JUDGE HOFFMAN: Do you approve of your client laughing out loud while the Court is making a decision on a motion made by them, sir?

WILLIAM KUNSTLER: I didn't hear it. I was talking to Mr. Davis.

JUDGE HOFFMAN: You seemed to be enjoying their laughter because you smiled yourself.

WILLIAM KUNSTLER: Your Honor, a smile is not forbidden in the federal court, I don't think.

JUDGE HOFFMAN: As long as you are putting things on the record, I think I will put on the record the posture of one of your clients. This is the United States district court. Have a look at him lying down there like he is on the ground. I won't discipline him at this time but I call attention to it on the record, as you put it.

WILLIAM KUNSTLER: It may reflect his attitude, your Honor, toward what is going on in the courtroom.

JUDGE HOFFMAN: Oh, I think it does. I think it does reflect his attitude.

WILLIAM KUNSTLER: Then it is free speech.

JUDGE HOFFMAN: And that attitude will be appropriately dealt with.

October 8, 1969

Government Witness Robert Pierson, undercover Chicago police officer

Pierson was one of three key government witnesses, Chicago police officers who had been undercover agents in the covert section of the Chicago Red Squad who had infiltrated the leadership of the demonstrations.

RICHARD SCHULTZ: Did you in any way alter your physical appearance to conduct your assignment as undercover investigator?

ROBERT PIERSON: Yes I did. I allowed my hair to grow long. I allowed myself to go without a shave for approximately four to six weeks. I purchased the attire of a motorcycle gang member, which is motorcycle boots, a black T-shirt, black Levis, and a black leather vest and a motorcycle helmet.

Q: Did you obtain a motorcycle?

A: Yes, I rented a motorcycle.

Q: Monday, August 26, 1968, did you have occasion on that day to go to Lincoln Park?

A: Yes sir, I did. Jordan introduced me to Abbie Hoffman. He said, "Abbie, this is Bob. He will be one of your bodyguards." I said to Hoffman that last night's confrontation was a pretty good one. And Hoffman said to me that "last night, they pushed us out of the park, but tonight, we're going to hold the park." He then said that, "we're going to—" and he used a foul word, "f—— up the pigs and the convention."

Q: What was the word, please, will you relate it?

A: He said "fuck."

Q: Then what did he say, please?

A: He said that, "If they push us out of the park tonight, we're going to break windows," and again he used a foul word.

Q: The same word?

A: Yes. And he said, "We're going to f—— up the North Side."

Q: What did you say when Hoffman told you this, please?

A: I told him that he could count on me helping him in every way in doing my best to keep him from being arrested.

October 10, 1969

Cross-examination about the events of Wednesday, August 28

LEONARD WEINGLASS: Were these policemen armed?

ROBERT PIERSON: Well, all uniformed police officers are armed.

Q: What where they armed with?

A: From what I could see, they had their standard equipment.

Q: Will you describe what they had in their hands as they went into that crowd?

A: They had batons.

Q: How were they holding their batons? Could you indicate that to the jury?

A: [*Indicating*] When the wedge first started coming into the crowd, they were holding their batons, I believe, with both hands.

Q: And did they then begin to use their batons?

A: Yes, sir, I believe they did.

Q: With one hand?

A: Yes, sir.

Q: In a swinging fashion?

A: Yes, sir.

Q: Striking people in front of them?

A: Yes, sir.

Q: Did you see anyone get hit on the head with a baton?

A: I saw clubs swung at people's heads, yes.

Q: By policemen?

A: Yes.

Q: They were swinging their clubs over their heads and down on the demonstrators?

A: Yes, sir.

October 13, 1969

Government Witness Detective Frank Riggio, Chicago Police Department

THOMAS FORAN: Calling your attention to August of 1968 during the Convention, were you given any specific assignment?

A: Yes, I was.

Q: What was that?

A: I was to keep Rennie Davis under surveillance.

Q: What was your tour of duty at the time?

A: I started at two in the afternoon and finished at two in the morning.

LEONARD WEINGLASS: At this point, this witness having identified himself now as a surveillance agent, on behalf of the defendant Rennie Davis I make the objection that a twenty-four-hour surveillance constitutes a constitutional invasion of a citizen's privacy contrary to the Fourteenth Amendment and I object to this witness being permitted to give any testimony in a court of law on the ground that his conduct constituted a violation of the United States Constitution.

JUDGE HOFFMAN: I will overrule the objection.

October 14, 1969

Defense attorney William Kunstler moved that court recess on Wednesday, October 15, 1969, to allow the defendants to participate in Moratorium Day antiwar protests.

WILLIAM KUNSTLER: I think it is as important, your Honor, to protest more than some thirty thousand American deaths and Lord knows how many Vietnamese deaths that have occurred in that country as it is to mourn one man in the United States, and if courts can close for the death of one man who lived a full life, they ought to close for the deaths of thousands and millions of innocent people whose lives have been corrupted and rotted and perverted by this utter horror that goes on in your name and my name—

JUDGE HOFFMAN: Not in my name.

WILLIAM KUNSTLER: It is in your name, too, in the name of the people of the United States.

JUDGE HOFFMAN: You just include yourself. Don't join me with you. Goodness. Don't you and I—

WILLIAM KUNSTLER: You are me, your Honor, because every citizen—you are a citizen the way I am a citizen.

JUDGE HOFFMAN: Only because you are a member of the bar of this Court and I am obligated to hear you respectfully as I have done.

WILLIAM KUNSTLER: No, your Honor, you are more than that. You are a citizen of the United States.

JUDGE HOFFMAN: Yes, I am.

WILLIAM KUNSTLER: And I am a citizen of the United States, and it is done in our name, in Judge Hoffman's name and William Kunstler's name.

JUDGE HOFFMAN: That will be all, sir. I shall hear you no further.

BOBBY SEALE: How come I can't speak in behalf of myself? I am my own legal counsel. I don't want these lawyers to represent me.

JUDGE HOFFMAN: You have a lawyer of record and he has been of record here since the twenty-fourth.

BOBBY SEALE: I have been arguing that before the jury heard one shred of evidence. I don't want these lawyers because I can take up my own legal defense and my lawyer is Charles Garry.

JUDGE HOFFMAN: Let the record show that the defendant Seale continued to speak after the Court courteously requested him to remain quiet.

October 15, 1969

Millions of Americans demonstrated against the war at "Vietnam Moratorium Day" protests in cities across the country. Nixon's vice president, Spiro Agnew, declared that Moratorium Day had been "encouraged by an effete corps of impudent snobs"—a line written by Nixon speechwriter William Safire, who later became a New York Times *op-ed page columnist. In court, the defendants attempted to observe Moratorium Day by placing American and South Vietnamese flags on the defense table and reading the names of war dead.*

DAVE DELLINGER: Mr. Hoffman, we are observing the Moratorium.

JUDGE HOFFMAN: I am Judge Hoffman, sir.

DAVE DELLINGER: I believe in equality, sir, so I prefer to call people Mr. or by their first name.

JUDGE HOFFMAN: Sit down. The clerk is about to call my cases.

Dave Dellinger

DAVE DELLINGER: I wanted to explain to you we are reading the names of the war dead.

THE MARSHAL: Sit down.

DAVE DELLINGER: We were just reading the names of the dead from both sides.

WILLIAM KUNSTLER: Your Honor, the defendants for the Vietnam moratorium brought in an American flag and a North Vietnamese flag which they placed on the counsel table to commemorate the dead Americans and the dead Vietnamese in this long and brutal war that has been going on. The marshal removed those from the table. First he took the North Vietnamese flag after directing me to order the client to have it removed, which I refused to do, and then he removed it himself, and then subsequently—I said North Vietnamese; I mean South Vietnamese, your Honor—he removed the American flag.

JUDGE HOFFMAN: We have an American flag in the corner. Haven't you seen it during the three-and-a-half weeks you have been here?

WILLIAM KUNSTLER: Yes, but we wanted the juxtaposition, your Honor, of the two flags together in one place.

JUDGE HOFFMAN: Mr. Kunstler, let me interrupt you to say that whatever decoration there is in the courtroom will be furnished by the government and I think things look all right in this courtroom.

WILLIAM KUNSTLER: Your Honor, I am applying for permission to have both flags on this Vietnam Moratorium Day.

JUDGE HOFFMAN: That permission will be denied. That is a table for the defendants and their lawyers and it is not to be decorated. We are not going to have the North Vietnamese flag on the table, sir.

ABBIE HOFFMAN: We don't consider this table a part of the Court and we want to furnish it in our own way.

THE MARSHAL: Sit down.

THOMAS FORAN:Your Honor, that is outrageous. This man [*Kunstler*] is a mouthpiece. Look at him, wearing a[n arm] band like his clients, your Honor. Any lawyer who comes into a courtroom and has no respect for the Court and acts in conjunction with that kind of a conduct before the Court, your Honor, the Government protests his attitude and would like to cite—to move the Court to make note of his conduct before this Court.

WILLIAM KUNSTLER: I am wearing an armband in memoriam to the dead, your Honor, which is no disgrace in this country. I want him admonished, your Honor. I request that you do that. The word "mouthpiece" is a contemptuous term.

JUDGE HOFFMAN: Did you say you want to admonish me?

WILLIAM KUNSTLER: No, I want you to admonish him.

JUDGE HOFFMAN: Let the record show I do not admonish the United States Attorney because he was properly representing his client, the United States of America.

WILLIAM KUNSTLER: Are you turning down my request after this disgraceful episode? You are not going to say anything?

JUDGE HOFFMAN: I not only turn it down, I ignore it.

October 17, 1969

JUDGE HOFFMAN: Ladies and gentlemen of the jury, good morning. Mr. Feinglass, will you please continue with the cross-examination of this witness?

WILLIAM KUNSTLER: Your Honor, so the record may be clear, I don't think Mr. Weinglass noticed the Feinglass. It is Mr. Weinglass.

JUDGE HOFFMAN: Oh, I did misspeak myself. I said Feinglass. I correct myself. I meant Weinglass. I am sorry I worked an F in there instead of the W that you deserve, Mr. Weinglass.

WILLIAM KUNSTLER: Mr. Oklepek, did you tell the grand jury anything about guns emanating from Mr. Hayden's mouth?

JUDGE HOFFMAN: That question will look awfully bad on paper, Mr. Kunstler. Nobody objected to it, but I just want you to have a good record.

WILLIAM KUNSTLER: I bow to your grammatical comments, and I withdraw the question and will ask you another.

JUDGE HOFFMAN: I just wanted you to know too I was listening to you.

WILLIAM KUNSTLER: I understand, your Honor. I have never doubted for a moment that you were listening.

Government Witness Carl Gilman, newsman and FBI informer

Gilman was one of several newsmen who worked as government informers, infuriating other journalists who saw their profession undermined and their own integrity as independent observers damaged. Gilman was a cameraman for a San Diego TV station who had also been working as an FBI informer and received $150 a month from the Bureau. He heard Dave Dellinger speak on July 25, 1968, at a rally at San Diego State College.

RICHARD SCHULTZ: Will you relate to the Court and the jury the last part, the very last part of the speech which Mr. Dellinger gave?

LEONARD WEINGLASS: If your Honor please, I object to this question. I object to this witness relating any speech given by a person before an open public rally at a college campus as being in violation of the First Amendment.

JUDGE HOFFMAN: Over the objection of the defendant, I will permit the witness to answer.

CARL GILMAN: [Dellinger said] "Burn your draft cards. Resist the draft. Violate the laws. Go to jail. Disrupt the United States government in any way you can to stop this insane war."

RICHARD SCHULTZ: Now, when he said that, what, if anything, occurred?

CARL GILMAN: The audience applauded. People stood up and whistled and yelled and screamed. They were very excited.

RICHARD SCHULTZ: If the Court please, if the marshals would—it is very disrupting to have the audience laughing during the court proceedings.

JUDGE HOFFMAN: I direct the marshals to admonish the spectators that they will be asked to leave if they do not refrain from noisy laughter.

RICHARD SCHULTZ: All right, as soon as he finished saying, "Disrupt the United States, stop the insane war," what occurred?

CARL GILMAN: As the applause died down, Mr. Dellinger said something and I missed the first word of perhaps the first two words, and after that he said, "I am going to Chicago to the Democratic National Convention where there may be problems." Then the audience applauded, stood up and yelled and screamed and whistled.

LEONARD WEINGLASS: If your Honor please, I renew my objection at this point. There is no mention of Mr. Dellinger's intention to commit any crime, either directly or indirectly in the city of Chicago from what I heard, so I don't think the speech as given by this witness even passes muster under the prosecutor's test.

JUDGE HOFFMAN: I thought I heard the witness testify about burning draft cards.

WILLIAM KUNSTLER: That is not what he is being prosecuted for, your Honor, for burning draft cards, for encouraging the burning of draft cards.

JUDGE HOFFMAN: You are right about that.

WILLIAM KUNSTLER: So it should be stricken; you agree with me?

JUDGE HOFFMAN: Oh, no. No, I shall not interpret his speech.

That is the responsibility of the jury. But I deny Leonard Weinglass's motion.

WILLIAM KUNSTLER: Your Honor, is someone being removed from the courtroom? Again another black person, I see.

RICHARD SCHULTZ: Say—this repeated comment about "another black person"—

A SPECTATOR: You hate black people or something?

RICHARD SCHULTZ: This constant repetition is not warranted, this attempt to make it appear that there is racism in this courtroom. And that response, your Honor, is so outrageous—it is so wrong and it is so deliberate by these men, it must stop. It is they who are engendering and who are looking for racism.

WILLIAM KUNSTLER: Your Honor, it's only been black people ejected that I have seen. I have never seen a white person removed from this courtroom when I have turned around, and this makes about the eleventh black person that's been—

JUDGE HOFFMAN: I don't know how from your position you can see what person has been ejected. I'm facing the door. I've never seen anybody ejected. I've seen people go out. I can't say that they were ejected, and I don't think that it is proper for a lawyer to refer to a person's race. And I direct you now, I order you now, not to refer to the ejection of a black person again.

WILLIAM KUNSTLER: I will not, your Honor, if black people are not constantly ejected from this Court.

October 20, 1969

The jury was excused.

THE CLERK: There is a motion here of defendant Bobby Seale pro se to be permitted to defend himself.

JUDGE HOFFMAN: I will hear you, Mr. Seale.

BOBBY SEALE: I want to present this motion in behalf of myself. I, Bobby Seale, demand and move the Court as follows: Because I am denied this lawyer of my choice, Charles R. Garry, I cannot represent myself as my attorney would be doing, but because I am forced to be my own counsel and to defend myself, I require my release from custody, from the bail presently in force, so that I can interview witnesses, do the necessary investigating, do necessary factual research and all other things that being in custody makes impossible. Two: The right to cross-examine witnesses and examine witnesses of my choice. Three: The right to make all necessary motions that I as a layman can think of to help my defense and prove my innocence and to argue those motions.

RICHARD SCHULTZ: May we briefly reply, your Honor? Your Honor, this is a ploy. It's just a simple obvious ploy.

JUDGE HOFFMAN: Mr. Seale has moved to be allowed to act as his own counsel and for relief on bail and ordered to perform certain functions he deems necessary to his defense. In exercising its discretion, the Court should deny a motion to defendant pro se when such procedure would be disruptive of the proceedings and when denial would not be prejudicial to the defendant. I find now that to allow the defendant Seale to act as his own attorney would produce the same disruptive effect. Moreover, the denial of the defendant's motion to appear pro se would not be prejudicial to his case. On the contrary, the complexity of the case makes self-representation inappropriate and the defendant would be more prejudiced were he allowed to conduct his own defense than if his motion were to be denied.

BOBBY SEALE: Now you are saying you are going to put me in

jail, you are going to put me in jail, that's one thing. You are going to put me in contempt of court because I am speaking in behalf of myself. The jury is prejudiced against me all right and you know it because of those threatening letters. You know it, those so-called jive threatening letters, and you know it's a lie. Now how can that jury give me a fair trial?

JUDGE HOFFMAN: Mr. Marshal will you go to that man and ask him to be quiet?

BOBBY SEALE: You know, the black man tries to get a fair trial in this country. The United States government, huh. Nixon and the rest of them. Go ahead and continue. I'll watch and get railroaded.

October 22, 1969

The jury was not present.

WILLIAM KUNSTLER: Mr. Seale informed me again on or about October 16th of this year that he was going to move before your Honor for permission to represent himself, and reiterated to me that he had discharged me and all other attorneys except Mr. Garry representing him, and that I should take no further action with reference to him and that I should withdraw formally. Accordingly, I am doing so through this motion which I have filed with your Honor yesterday, and a copy has been served upon the United States Attorney.

THOMAS FORAN: It is then subject to the sound discretion of the Court as to whether or not this prior right prior to the beginning of the trial of a client to defend himself is overcome in the Court's discretion by the strong likelihood that the discharge of a lawyer in the midst of a trial would result in total destruction of court proceedings—total disruption of court proceedings to the prejudice of a fair trial. On that basis, your Honor, the Government asks the Court to deny the motion.

A spectator was evicted from the courtroom.

BOBBY SEALE: You are a pig for kicking him out.

SPECTATORS: RIGHT ON, RIGHT ON!

THE MARSHAL: This Honorable Court will now resume its session.

THE SPECTATORS: OINK! OINK!

WILLIAM KUNSTLER: Your Honor, if I could make one application—the other seven defendants have purchased a birthday cake for Chairman Bobby Seale whose thirty-third birthday is today and they have requested me to ask your Honor's permission since the marshals would not let them bring the cake to Mr. Seale to at least bring it to him and present him with the cake before the jury comes in.

JUDGE HOFFMAN: Mr. Kunstler, I won't even let anybody bring me a birthday cake. I don't have food in my chambers. I don't have any beverages. This is a courthouse and we conduct trials here. I am sorry.

RENNIE DAVIS: They arrested your cake, Bobby. They arrested it.

October 23, 1969

Government Witness Louis Salzberg, journalist and FBI informer

Salzberg was a press photographer from New York City and a paid FBI informant who received "around seven, eight thousand dollars"

*from the Bureau. He was asked about a meeting at a church in Man-
hattan on March 14, 1968, where Tom Hayden spoke.*

RICHARD SCHULTZ: Would you relate exactly what he said?
A: He said it was the purpose of the National Mobilization
Committee to fuck up the Convention in Chicago.

Cross-examination

WILLIAM KUNSTLER: [In your report to the FBI], did you include the words that Mr. Hayden said?
A: No I did not. The agent related to me that any reports that I
was to phone in could not have any obscenities in it. They will
not print them, and I asked him why, and he told me that they
have young girls as stenographers, and they will not print
them that way.
Q: Was not a question asked of Mr. Hayden about violence in
Chicago?
A: The question was whether or not there would be summer violence in Chicago, rioting, and Hayden answered to that that he
hoped it would not be. It was not their purpose to excite any of
the black ghettoes to violence in Chicago.

Government Witness Frank D. Sweeney, adman and FBI
informer

*Sweeney was a New York advertising man who had been paid $300
by the FBI for reports on meetings. He testified about Tom Hayden's
statements at a meeting of the Fifth Avenue Peace Parade Committee
at a New York hotel on July 25, 1968.*

FRANK SWEENEY: [Tom Hayden] said that the war in Vietnam was immoral, it was a war of genocide and that the United States was an outlaw nation. He said that because the United States was an outlaw nation, it had broken all of the rules, and therefore the peace demonstrators could break all the rules, too. He specifically referred to the upcoming Democratic Convention in Chicago. He spoke about the fact that the North Vietnamese were shedding blood and the peace demonstrators when they went to Chicago should be prepared to shed blood, too.

Hayden later wrote that "what I had in fact said was that we had to be "prepared for shedding our own blood" and that the "rules of the game of politics were rigged and ought to be broken." [1]

October 27, 1969

BOBBY SEALE: What about my constitutional right to defend myself and have my lawyer?

JUDGE HOFFMAN: Your constitutional rights—

BOBBY SEALE: You are denying them. You have been denying them. Every other word you say is denied, denied, denied, denied, and you begin to oink in the faces of the masses of the people of this country. That is what you begin to represent, the corruptness of this rotten government of four hundred years—

THE MARSHAL: Mr. Seale, will you sit down?

BOBBY SEALE: Why don't you knock me in the mouth? Try that.

THE MARSHAL: Sit down.

JUDGE HOFFMAN: Ladies and gentlemen of the jury, I regret that I will have to excuse you.

BOBBY SEALE: I hope you don't blame me for anything and those false lying notes and letters that were sent that said the Black Panther Party threatened that jury, it's a lie, and you know it's a lie, and the government did it to taint the jury against me.

The jury was excused.

BOBBY SEALE: You got that? This racist administrative government with its Superman notions and comic-book politics. We're hip to the fact that Superman never saved no black people. You got that?

Government Witness William Frapolly, undercover Chicago police officer

Frapolly was a member of the Chicago Red Squad, and one of three key government witnesses. As a student at a state college, he grew his hair long and infiltrated SDS, the Mobe, and other antiwar groups. He was asked what Rennie Davis said at a meeting at the Mobe headquarters on August 9 at which the demonstrations were being planned.

WILLIAM FRAPOLLY: He said a mill-in would be to get anywhere from fifty to a hundred thousand people into the Loop, and then these people would go through the Loop and they would try and disrupt it. He said, "We would block cars driving down the street, we would block people coming and going out of buildings. We would run through stores. We would smash windows and generally try to shut the Loop down."

Frapolly was asked about a "Free Huey" rally in Lincoln Park on August 27, 1968.

THOMAS FORAN: Did you recognize any of the speakers?

A: I heard Jerry Rubin give a speech, Phil Ochs sang, and then a person who identified himself as Bobby Seale spoke.

BOBBY SEALE: I object to that because my lawyer is not here. I have been denied my right to defend myself in this courtroom. I object to this man's testimony against me because I have not been allowed my constitutional rights.

JUDGE HOFFMAN: I repeat to you, sir, you have a lawyer. Your lawyer is William Kunstler.

BOBBY SEALE: He does not represent me.

The jury was removed from courtroom.

JUDGE HOFFMAN: Now you just keep on this way and—

BOBBY SEALE: Keep on what? Keep on what? Keep on getting denied my constitutional rights?

JUDGE HOFFMAN: Will you be quiet?

BOBBY SEALE: Now I still object. I object because you know it is wrong. You denied me my right to defend myself. You think black people don't have a mind. Well, we got big minds, good minds, and we know how to come forth with constitutional rights. I still object to that man testifying against me without my lawyer being here, without me having a right to defend myself.

JUDGE HOFFMAN: Are you getting all of this, Miss Reporter?

BOBBY SEALE: I hope she gets it all.

October 28, 1969

BOBBY SEALE: I would like to request to cross-examine the witness.

JUDGE HOFFMAN: You have a lawyer here.

BOBBY SEALE: That man is not my lawyer. You are violating Title 42, United States Criminal Code. You are violating it because it states that a black man cannot be discriminated against in his legal defense. It is an old Reconstruction law and you won't recognize it, so I would like to cross-examine the witness.

THE MARSHAL: Sit down, Mr. Seale.

The jury was excused.

BOBBY SEALE: Hey, did you see me make a speech in Lincoln Park, William—Mr. William Frapolly?

JUDGE HOFFMAN: Let the record show that the defendant Seale keeps on talking without the approval of the Court and in spite of the admonition of Judge Hoffman and in contempt of the Court.

BOBBY SEALE: Let the record show you violated that and a black man cannot be discriminated against in relation to his legal defense and that is exactly what you have done.

JUDGE HOFFMAN: The record shows exactly to the contrary.

BOBBY SEALE: The record shows that you are violating, that you violated my constitutional rights. I want to cross-examine the witness.

JUDGE HOFFMAN: I admonish you, sir, that you have a lot of contemptuous conduct against you.

BOBBY SEALE: I admonish you. You are in contempt of people's constitutional rights.

TOM HAYDEN: Let the record show the judge was laughing.

BOBBY SEALE: Yes, he is laughing.

JUDGE HOFFMAN: Who made that remark?

THOMAS FORAN: The defendant Hayden, your Honor, made the remark.

BOBBY SEALE: And me.

JUDGE HOFFMAN: I am warning you, sir, that the law—

BOBBY SEALE: Instead of warning, why don't you warn me I have got a right to defend myself, huh?

JUDGE HOFFMAN: I am warning you that the Court has the right to gag you. I don't want to do that. Under the law you may be gagged and chained to your chair.

BOBBY SEALE: Gagged? I am being railroaded already.

JUDGE HOFFMAN: The Court has that right and I—

BOBBY SEALE: The Court has no right whatsoever. The court has no right to stop me from speaking out in behalf of my constitutional rights.

JUDGE HOFFMAN: The Court will be in recess until tomorrow morning at ten o'clock.

THE MARSHAL: Everyone will please rise.

BOBBY SEALE: I am not rising. I am not rising until he recognizes my constitutional rights.

JUDGE HOFFMAN: Mr. Marshal, see that he rises.

THE MARSHAL: Mr. Seale—

JUDGE HOFFMAN: And the other one, too. Get all of the defendants to rise.

THE MARSHAL: Mr. Hayden, will you please rise.

JUDGE HOFFMAN: Let the record show that none of the defendants has risen. The Court will be in recess.

October 29, 1969

ABBIE HOFFMAN: There are twenty-five marshals in here now, and they all got guns.

WILLIAM KUNSTLER: Your Honor, we are objecting to this

armed-camp aspect that is going on since the beginning of this trial.

JUDGE HOFFMAN: It is not an armed camp.

WILLIAM KUNSTLER: It is not right, and it's not good, and it's not called for.

RICHARD SCHULTZ: If the Court please, before you came into this courtroom, if the Court please, Bobby Seale stood up and addressed this group.

BOBBY SEALE: That's right, brother.

RICHARD SCHULTZ: And Bobby Seale said if he is—that if he's attacked, they know what to do.

BOBBY SEALE: I can speak on behalf of my constitutional rights, too.

RICHARD SCHULTZ: He was talking to these people about an attack by them.

BOBBY SEALE: You're lying. Dirty liar. I told them to defend themselves. You are a rotten racist pig, fascist liar, that's what you are. You're a rotten liar. You're a rotten liar. You are a fascist pig liar. I hope the record shows that tricky Dick Schultz, working for Richard Nixon and administration all understand that tricky Dick Schultz is a liar, and we have a right to defend ourselves, and if you attack me I will defend myself.

SPECTATORS: RIGHT ON!

BOBBY SEALE: A physical attack by those damned marshals, that's what I said.

JUDGE HOFFMAN: Let the record show the tone of Mr. Seale's voice was one shrieking and pounding on the table and shouting. That will be dealt with appropriately at some time in the future.

WILLIAM KUNSTLER: Your Honor, the record should indicate that Mr. Schultz shouted.

JUDGE HOFFMAN: If what he said was the truth, I can't blame him for raising his voice.

The jury was brought in, then excused.

JUDGE HOFFMAN: [*to Bobby Seale*] I will ask you to sit down, sir. You have a lawyer to speak for you. I haven't been told that you represent all of these defendants, either.

ABBIE HOFFMAN: We have been told that they are defendants, too.

JUDGE HOFFMAN: The last statement was made by the defendant Abbie Hoffman.

ABBIE HOFFMAN: I don't use that last name any more.

Cross-examination

LEONARD WEINGLASS: At that meeting [*another, two days earlier*] it was you who suggested that grappling hooks and ropes be used to stop jeeps which had barbed wire on the front of them, is that correct?

WILLIAM FRAPOLLY: That is not correct, sir.

Q: Tell us what you suggested to Rennie Davis?

A: I suggested to Rennie Davis and some other people that a grappling hook be thrown into barbed wire as it was being strung out from a truck.

Q: People were asking for suggestions but you were the only one who volunteered that a military vehicle should be sabotaged, isn't that true?

A: I think there were other suggestions, sir.

JUDGE HOFFMAN: Is there any redirect examination?

BOBBY SEALE: Before the redirect, I would like to request again—demand—that I be able to cross-examine the witness.

My lawyer is not here. I think I have a right to defend myself in this courtroom.

JUDGE HOFFMAN: Take the jury out.

BOBBY SEALE: You have George Washington and Benjamin Franklin sitting in a picture behind you, and they was slave owners. That's what they were. They owned slaves. You are acting in the same manner, denying me my constitutional rights being able to cross-examine this witness.

The jury was excused.

JUDGE HOFFMAN: Mr. Seale, I have admonished you previously—

BOBBY SEALE: I have a right to cross-examine the witness.

JUDGE HOFFMAN: —what might happen to you if you keep on talking. We are going to recess now, young man. If you keep this up—

BOBBY SEALE: Look, old man, if you keep up denying me my constitutional rights, you are being exposed to the public and the world that you do not care about people's constitutional rights to defend themselves.

JUDGE HOFFMAN: I will tell you that what I indicated yesterday might happen to you—

BOBBY SEALE: Happen to me? What can happen to me more than what Benjamin Franklin and George Washington did to black people in slavery? What can happen to me more than that?

JUDGE HOFFMAN: [*to William Kunstler*] Now, I will tell you this, that since it has been said here that all of the defendants support this man in what he is doing, I over the noon hour will reflect on whether they are good risks for bail and I shall give serious consideration to the termination of their bail if you can't control your clients.

WILLIAM KUNSTLER: Your Honor, they said they supported fully his right to defend himself or have his lawyer of choice, and if that is the price of their bail, then I guess that will have to be the price of their bail.

BOBBY SEALE: Can I say something to the Court?

JUDGE HOFFMAN: No, thank you.

BOBBY SEALE: Why not?

JUDGE HOFFMAN: Well, I have been called a racist, a fascist— he has pointed to the picture of George Washington behind me and called him a slave owner and—

BOBBY SEALE: They were slave owners. Look at history.

JUDGE HOFFMAN: As though I had anything to do with that.

BOBBY SEALE: They were slave owners. You got them up there.

JUDGE HOFFMAN: He has been known as the father of this country, and I would think that it is a pretty good picture to have in the United States district court.

WILLIAM KUNSTLER: We all share a common guilt, your Honor.

JUDGE HOFFMAN: I didn't think I would ever live to sit on a bench or be in a courtroom where George Washington was assailed by a defendant in a criminal case and a judge was criticized for having his portrait on the wall.

BOBBY SEALE: What about Section 1982, Title 42 of the Code where it says the black man cannot be discriminated against in my legal defense in any court in America?

JUDGE HOFFMAN: Mr. Seale, do you want to stop or do you want me to direct the marshal—

BOBBY SEALE: I want to argue the point.

JUDGE HOFFMAN: We will take a recess. Take that defendant

into the room there and deal with him as he should be dealt with in this circumstance.

BOBBY SEALE: I still want to be represented. I want to represent myself.

THE MARSHAL: William Kunstler, will you instruct the defendants, sir, that it is the order of the Court that they will arise upon the recess?

WILLIAM KUNSTLER: If that is a direction of the Court, I certainly will pass it on.

JUDGE HOFFMAN: Let the record show none of the defendants have stood at this recess in response to the marshal's request.

BOBBY SEALE: Let the record show that—

THE MARSHAL: This Court will now take a brief recess.

BOBBY SEALE: Let the record show—

At this point, half a dozen marshals dragged Bobby Seale away, and all of the defendants jumped out of their seats. Dave Dellinger tried to protect Seale, but was knocked down. Jerry Rubin yelled, "They're kicking him in the balls," and then was punched in the face by a marshal. Tom Hayden shouted to the judge, "Your Honor, all he wants is to be legally represented, not be a slave here."

Hayden described what happened next: "No one in court that day will ever forget the loathsome sight of Bobby Seale being carried back into the room. Surrounded by marshals, he was sitting in a high chair with his wrists and ankles strapped under clanking chains. Wrapped around his mouth and back of his head was a thick white cloth. His eyes and the veins in his neck and temples were bulging with the strain of maintaining his breath. As shocking as the chains and gag were, even more unbelievable was the attempt to return the courtroom to normalcy."[2] The jury returned and the prosecutor addressed the judge.

Bobby Seale bound and gagged

THOMAS FORAN: Your Honor, if Mr. Seale would express to the Court his willingness to be quiet, would the Court entertain the possibility under those circumstances of Mr. Seale being unbound and ungagged?

JUDGE HOFFMAN: I have tried so hard, with all my heart, to get him to sit in this Court and be tried fairly and impartially, and I have been greeted on every occasion with all sorts of vicious invective. Mr. Seale, I ask you, and you may indicate, by raising your head up and down or shaking your head, meaning no, whether or not I have your assurance that you will not do anything that will disrupt this trial if you are permitted to resume your former place at the table. Will you, sir?

To the amazement of all, Seale was able to speak in a muffled voice through his gag, and the court stenographer recorded his words.

BOBBY SEALE [*gagged*]: I can't speak. I have a right to speak. I have a right to speak and be heard for myself and my constitutional rights.

WILLIAM KUNSTLER: I wanted to say the record should indicate that Mr. Seale is seated on a metal chair, each hand is handcuffed to the leg of the chair on both the right and left sides so he cannot raise his hands, and a gag is tightly pressed into his mouth and tied at the rear, and that when he attempts to speak, a muffled sound comes out as he has done several times since he has been bound and gagged.

BOBBY SEALE [*gagged*]: You don't represent me. Sit down, Kunstler.

JUDGE HOFFMAN: Mr. Marshal, I don't think you have accomplished your purpose by that kind of a contrivance. We will have to take another recess.

At this point the marshals carried Bobby Seale in his chair out of the courtroom and then brought him back with what Tom Hayden later described as "a pluglike device" in his mouth tied around his face with the cloth gag.[3] *The judge then tried to explain this horrifying spectacle to the jury.*

JUDGE HOFFMAN: Ladies and gentlemen of the jury, I must tell you that in a trial by jury in a federal court in the United States, the judge is not a mere moderator under the law but is the governor of the trial for the purpose of assuring its proper conduct, and fairness, and for the purpose of determining questions of law. The law requires that the judge maintain order and to take

Bobby Seale bound and gagged

such steps as in the discretion of the judge are warranted, and, accordingly, the marshals have endeavored to maintain order in the manner that you see here in the courtroom. Mr. Weinglass, do you wish to cross-examine the witness?

WILLIAM KUNSTLER: Your Honor, before Mr. Foran proceeds, I just want to move for the other seven defendants other than Mr. Seale for the removal of the irons and the gag on the ground that he was attempting only to assert this right to self-defense under the Constitution and I move on behalf of the other seven defendants for the immediate removal of the gag and the arm and leg cuffs.

JUDGE HOFFMAN: Mr. Kunstler has made a motion in behalf of the seven other defendants. I direct you, ladies and gentlemen of the jury, to not hold it against any of the seven other defendants when these measures are taken with respect to the defendant Mr. Seale. These measures indicate no evidence of his guilt or lack of guilt of the charges contained in the indictment. These measures have been taken only, as I say, to insure the proper conduct of this trial which I am obligated to do under the law. The motion of Mr. Kunstler will be denied.

October 30, 1969

Bobby Seale again appeared before the jury bound and gagged. Testimony began, but the judge quickly ordered the jury from the courtroom. A group of marshals began struggling with Seale and kicked his chair over. Everyone jumped up, and according to Tom Hayden's memoir, "marshals were slugging and elbowing the other defendants, spectators, and even members of the press."[*]

WILLIAM KUNSTLER: Your Honor, are we going to stop this medieval torture that is going on in this courtroom? I think this is a disgrace.

JERRY RUBIN: This guy is putting his elbow in Bobby's mouth and it wasn't necessary at all.

WILLIAM KUNSTLER: This is no longer a court of order, your Honor, this is a medieval torture chamber. It is a disgrace. They are assaulting the other defendants also.

JERRY RUBIN: Don't hit me in my balls, motherfucker.

BOBBY SEALE [*gagged*]: This motherfucker is tight and it is stopping my blood.

WILLIAM KUNSTLER: Your Honor, this is an unholy disgrace to the law that is going on in this courtroom and I as an American lawyer feel a disgrace.

THOMAS FORAN: Created by Mr. Kunstler.

WILLIAM KUNSTLER: Created by nothing other than what you have done to this man.

ABBIE HOFFMAN: You come down here and watch it, Judge.

THOMAS FORAN: May the record show that the outbursts are the defendant Rubin.

BOBBY SEALE [*gagged*]: You fascist dogs, you rotten low-life son of a bitch. I am glad I said it about Washington used to have slaves, the first president—

WILLIAM KUNSTLER: I just feel so utterly ashamed to be an American lawyer at this time.

JUDGE HOFFMAN: You should be ashamed of your conduct in this case, sir.

WILLIAM KUNSTLER: What conduct, when a client is treated in this manner?

JUDGE HOFFMAN: We will take a brief recess.

WILLIAM KUNSTLER: Can we have somebody with Mr. Seale? We don't trust—

JUDGE HOFFMAN: He is not your client, you said.

WILLIAM KUNSTLER: We are speaking for the other seven [defendants].

JUDGE HOFFMAN: The marshals will take care of him.

JERRY RUBIN: Take care of him?

After a recess, the judge instructed Weinglass to continue a cross-examination.

LEONARD WEINGLASS: Standing here at this lectern as I am just five feet from a man who is shackled and gagged and bound and who, when the jury is not in this courtroom—

JUDGE HOFFMAN: Will you continue with your cross-examination?

LEONARD WEINGLASS: —is physically assaulted by the marshals—I am attempting to explain why it is impossible for me at this point to proceed with my cross-examination of this witness. I would like to ask the Court as a motion of the defendants to poll the jury to see whether or not the jurors feel that they can continue in this case with orderly deliberations while one man is sitting here receiving the treatment that Bobby Seale is being given in this courtroom.

The jury was excused.

JUDGE HOFFMAN: The form of the motion is bad, therefore I deny it.

LEONARD WEINGLASS: May I have an opportunity to rephrase the form of the motion?

JUDGE HOFFMAN: No.

The jury returned to the courtroom.

JUDGE HOFFMAN: Ladies and gentlemen of the jury, these incidents are not to be considered by you in determining the guilt or innocence of any of the defendants and I order you to disregard the incidents. Mr. Seale, I order you to refrain from making those noises.

RENNIE DAVIS: Ladies and gentlemen of the jury, he was being tortured while you were out of this room by these marshals. They come and torture him while you are out of the room. It is a terrible thing what is happening.

The judge ordered the jury removed.

TOM HAYDEN: Now they are going to beat him, they are going to beat him.

ABBIE HOFFMAN: You may as well kill him if you are going to gag him.

JUDGE HOFFMAN: You are not permitted to address the Court, Mr. Hoffman. You have a lawyer.

ABBIE HOFFMAN: This isn't a court. This is a neon oven. [*Hoffman was referring to the courtroom ceiling, a massive array of fluorescent lights.*] The disruption started when these guys got into overkill. It is the same thing as last year in Chicago, the same exact thing.

JUDGE HOFFMAN: Mr. Seale, I would like to get your assurance that there will be no repetition of the conduct engaged in by you this morning. Let the record show that the defendant did not reply in the manner—in which I asked.

LEONARD WEINGLASS: If your Honor please, Mr. Seale can't answer the Court verbally since his mouth is also gagged and so I would like to read and then offer into the record as an exhibit the following note which Mr. Seale has written. "I want and demand my right to defend myself, to be able to object acting as my own defense counsel, to be able to continue to argue my motions and requests as any defendant or citizen of America."

JUDGE HOFFMAN: It may be marked as an exhibit.

October 31, 1969

The trial resumed with Bobby Seale again bound and gagged.

LEONARD WEINGLASS: If your Honor please, Mr. Seale is having difficulty. The marshal has noticed it. He is in extreme discomfort. He has written me a note that the circulation of blood in his head is stopped by the pressure of the bandage on the top of the skull and would it be possible to have those bandages loosened? He is breathing very heavily. I think both marshals can note it.

WILLIAM KUNSTLER: I would like to reiterate I am calling for an end of this. I think this is absolutely medieval. I don't think you have seen it in your experience nor I have seen it in mine.

JUDGE HOFFMAN: The record does not indicate that I could stop Mr. Seale.

WILLIAM KUNSTLER: You can, your Honor. He asks one thing of you and that is the right to defend himself.

JUDGE HOFFMAN: You are his lawyer and if you were any kind of a lawyer you would continue to do it.

WILLIAM KUNSTLER: If I were any kind of a lawyer I would protest against what is being done in this courtroom and I am so protesting on behalf of the other seven defendants in this case.

JUDGE HOFFMAN: Why should I have to go through a trial and be assailed in an obscene manner?

WILLIAM KUNSTLER: But, your Honor, that is a reaction of a black man to not being permitted to defend himself. If you had said to him, "Defend yourself," none of this would have happened.

JUDGE HOFFMAN: I have had black lawyers in this courtroom who tried cases with dignity and with ability. His color has nothing to do with his conduct.

WILLIAM KUNSTLER: We feel as attorneys and so do the seven other defendants that it is impossible to continue as human beings with the trial of this case under the present circumstances: that it is impossible for essentially white men to sit in this room while a black man is in chains and continue—

JUDGE HOFFMAN: I wish you wouldn't talk about the distinction between white and black men in this courtroom.

WILLIAM KUNSTLER: A lot of the seven white men.

JUDGE HOFFMAN: I lived a long time and you are the first person who has ever suggested that I have discriminated against a black man. Come into my chambers and I will show you on the wall what one of the great newspapers of the city said editorially about me in connection with [a] school segregation case.

WILLIAM KUNSTLER: Your Honor, this is not a time for self-praise on either side of the lectern.

JUDGE HOFFMAN: It isn't self-praise, sir. It is defense. I won't let a lawyer stand before the bar and charge me with being a bigot.

WILLIAM KUNSTLER: For God's sake, your Honor, we are seeking a solution of a human problem here, not whether you feel good or bad or I feel good or bad.

JUDGE HOFFMAN: Oh, of course not. I think that it is just very pleasant for a judge to sit up here and be called a fascist, racist—I couldn't begin to recite all of the things that this man has said.

November 3, 1969

When the trial resumed after a weekend break, Bobby Seale was sitting in his chair, without gag or chains. Apparently the spectacle on national TV of a black man bound and gagged in a federal courtroom was too damaging to the government's case. Tom Hayden recalled that, as the day began, Weinglass whispered to him at the defense table, "They've decided to get rid of [Seale]. It'll be a mistrial."[5] It took two more days.

LEONARD WEINGLASS: Can't Mr. Schultz understand that a man is sitting here on trial facing the possibility of a ten-year jail sentence without his attorney being in this courtroom?

November 4, 1969

BOBBY SEALE: I wasn't shackled because I called you a pig and a fascist, which I still think you are, a pig, and a fascist, and a racist, but I was denied my constitutional rights. When a man is denied his constitutional rights—
JUDGE HOFFMAN: Will you sit down, please.
BOBBY SEALE: —in the manner that you did—
JUDGE HOFFMAN: Mr. Marshal, have that man sit down.
BOBBY SEALE: —you will still be considered a pig, and a fascist, and a racist by me. You still denied me my constitutional rights.
JUDGE HOFFMAN: Miss Reporter, did you get Mr. Seale's remarks?

November 5, 1969

Government Witness Bill H. Ray, deputy sheriff, San Mateo County

Ray was called by the prosecution to testify that he saw Bobby Seale on August 27, 1968, at San Francisco airport, boarding a flight for Chicago. The testimony was necessary because the indictment had charged "interstate travel."

JUDGE HOFFMAN: Are you ready to proceed with the cross-examination, gentlemen of the Defense side?

BOBBY SEALE: Yeah.

JUDGE HOFFMAN: Mr. Kunstler, do you have any cross-examination of this witness?

WILLIAM KUNSTLER: Your Honor, since this witness only related facts relevant to Mr. Seale who has, as your Honor knows, discharged me, I have no questions.

BOBBY SEALE: I think I have a right to cross-examine.

JUDGE HOFFMAN: Mr. Seale, I ask you to sit down.

BOBBY SEALE: Have you ever killed a Black Panther Party member?

JUDGE HOFFMAN: Mr. Seale, I will have to ask you to sit down, please.

BOBBY SEALE: Have you ever been on any raids in the Black Panther Party's offices or Black Panther Party members' homes?

JUDGE HOFFMAN: Mr. Seale, this is the third time I am asking you to sit down as courteously as possible.

The jury was excused, and the judge ordered a recess until afternoon.

JUDGE HOFFMAN: As we all know, the defendant Bobby G. Seale has been guilty of conduct in the presence of the Court during this trial which is not only contumacious in character but of so grave a character as to continually disrupt the orderly administration of justice.

BOBBY SEALE: That is a lie. I stood up and spoke in behalf of myself and made motions and requests. I stood up and walked to the lectern and demonstrated the fact I wanted to cross-examine the witness.

JUDGE HOFFMAN: You are making it very difficult for me, Mr. Seale.

BOBBY SEALE: You are making it difficult for me, Judge Hoffman.

JUDGE HOFFMAN: The Court also notes that a reading of the record cannot and does not reflect the true intensity and extent of the disruption which in some instances were accompanied by physical violence—

BOBBY SEALE: That is a lie.

JUDGE HOFFMAN: —which occurred in the presence of the Court.

BOBBY SEALE: That is a lie. I never attacked anyone and you know it. I never struck anyone and you know it.

JUDGE HOFFMAN: I find that the acts, statements and conduct of the defendant Bobby Seale constituted a deliberate and willful attack upon the administration of justice, an attempt to sabotage the functioning of the federal judiciary system, and misconduct of so grave a character as to make the mere imposition of a fine a futile gesture and a wholly insignificant punishment. Accordingly, I adjudged Bobby G. Seale guilty of each and every specification referred to in my oral observations, and

That is a lie. I never attacked anyone and you know it. I never struck anyone and you know it.

Bobby Seale and Judge Hoffman

the Court will impose—strike that—and the defendant Seale will be committed to the custody of the Attorney General of the United States or his authorized representative for imprisonment for a term of three months on each and every specification, the sentences to run consecutively.

Judge Hoffman listed sixteen incidents for which Bobby Seale was sentenced for contempt; the sentences totaled four years.

JUDGE HOFFMAN: There will be an order declaring a mistrial as to the defendant Bobby G. Seale and not as to any other defendants.

BOBBY SEALE: Wait a minute, I got a right—what's the cat trying to pull now? I can't stay? I still want an immediate trial. You can't call it a mistrial. I'm put in jail for four years for nothing? I want my coat.

SPECTATORS: Free Bobby! Free Bobby!

The marshals then took Bobby Seale off to prison.

The severance of Bobby Seale and his sentencing for contempt for demanding the right to defend himself marked the conclusion of the most dramatic weeks in any American political trial in half a century. It also turned the trial of the Chicago Eight into the trial of the Chicago Seven.

November 6, 1969

LEONARD WEINGLASS: If the Court please, we have an oral motion for a mistrial.

JUDGE HOFFMAN: A what?

WILLIAM KUNSTLER: May it please the Court, we have here a very fundamental issue. The severance out and the mistrial, as

Bobby Seale

to Bobby Seale, come much too late in the game. Your Honor, there is a violation of basic American constitutional rights which is so fundamental that we feel it makes this entire proceeding null and void. We urge your Honor to grant the mistrial for all defendants remaining in this case.

JUDGE HOFFMAN: Based on the record in this case and the applicable authorities which the Court has examined prior to coming in here this morning, the motion of the seven other defendants for a mistrial will be denied.

Government Witness John Braddock, news cameraman for ABC-TV

Braddock filmed a speech by Tom Hayden in Grant Park early the morning of Wednesday, August 28. The film was shown to the jury without objection by the defense.

TOM HAYDEN [*on film*]: We have found that our primary struggle has not been to expose the bankruptcy of the Democratic Party. They have done that for themselves. Our primary struggle is our struggle for our own survival, for our own survival as a movement, for our own survival as an emerging culture facing military suppression at every step of its emergence.

A final point addressed to the people inside the hotel and the people who have come from the hotel to be with us here. What would be very good, I believe, what would be very good for you to do in the morning is welcome us into the hotel, into your rooms, more particularly into your bathrooms so that we can clean up because we have a lot of work to do tomorrow.

Tomorrow is the day that this operation has been pointing toward for some time. We see before us at this hour the realities of American society exposed before us, daring us to take a step. But we are going to take the step. We are going to gather here. We are going to make our way to the Amphitheatre by any means necessary.

November 7, 1969

Attorney Francis I. McTernan argued against Seale's four-year sentence imposed by Judge Hoffman for contempt.

FRANCIS MCTERNAN: Here is a layman, not trained as a lawyer, asking for what he considered his right to defend himself and discharge lawyers of record because the lawyer of his choice was not here.

JUDGE HOFFMAN: You can disagree with the judge, laymen or lawyers—

FRANCIS MCTERNAN: A layman is not a lawyer.

JUDGE HOFFMAN: —but you don't call him a pig and a fascist in the process of disagreeing with him.

FRANCIS MCTERNAN: What I wanted to get to is this: You keep referring back to how contemptuous the conduct was and I am trying to say to your Honor, and I would like to develop the argument because I didn't get it all out, that we were dealing first with a layman and not a lawyer. Secondly, we were dealing with a black man who comes out of a black ghetto.

JUDGE HOFFMAN: Oh, I don't want to hear another thing about a black man. The only person who mentioned black men in this Court for the first time was your client. You don't know me, sir, but I am as good a friend of the black people in this community as they have, and if you don't believe it, read the books.

FRANCIS MCTERNAN: I am not suggesting, your Honor, in this phase of my argument that he was discriminated against.

JUDGE HOFFMAN: Then why mention color?

FRANCIS MCTERNAN: Because it has to do with the words he used, your Honor. It has to do with the culture from which he comes and the meaning ascribed to words. That is what I want to address myself to.

JUDGE HOFFMAN: I have known literally thousands of what we used to call Negro people, and who are now referred to as black people, and I never heard that kind of language emanate from the lips of any one of them. I have had fine Negro lawyers stand

I'm about as good a friend of the black people in this community as they have.

Judge Hoffman

at that lectern and at the lectern across in the old courthouse, and I never heard a lawyer, a Negro lawyer use that kind of language, or any Negro witness, or any Negro defendant in a criminal case. I never did. There is no evidence here in this case that it is part of a culture.

THOMAS FORAN: I would call something else to the Court's attention which again makes counsel's motion really moot and that is that Mr. Seale is not only under a charge but that he is under a charge in New Haven, Connecticut, for conspiracy to commit murder. He is not entitled to be on the street even under the Constitution. There is no one in this courtroom that does not know that Mr. Seale is a highly intelligent and articulate man. The idea, the very idea that his gross conduct in this courtroom was due to his race is an insult to any human being who is a member of that race. His gross conduct was because he acted contemptuously in this Court, he as a human being.

November 12, 1969

Government Witness Irwin Bock, undercover Chicago police officer

Bock was a member of the "covert" section of the Chicago Red Squad, and one of three star witnesses for the government. A navy veteran, he had infiltrated Veterans for Peace, then infiltrated the steering committee of the Mobilization, and then became a demonstration marshal during the convention. He was on the witness stand from November 12 to 20. He was asked by Richard Schultz to describe a meeting at the Mobilization office on August 9 at which demonstrations at the upcoming convention were planned.

IRWIN BOCK: Hayden said that he, Rennie Davis, and Abbie Hoffman had been making plans for diversionary tactics to take place while the main march was going to the Amphitheatre. These diversionary tactics were the breaking of windows, pulling of fire-alarm boxes, the setting of small fires, and that they had two purposes. Tom Hayden said that if the South and West Sides would rise up as they did in the April riots in Chicago here, the city would have a lot of trouble on their hands.

November 18, 1989

JUDGE HOFFMAN: Mr. Kunstler, there is a great architect, Mies van der Rohe, who lately left us. He designed that lectern as well as this building and it was a lectern, not a leaning post. I have asked you to stand behind it when you question the witness.

WILLIAM KUNSTLER: Your Honor, the U.S. Attorney questions from the back of this table and leans on his material.

JUDGE HOFFMAN: I don't care about that.

WILLIAM KUNSTLER: Why am I different?

JUDGE HOFFMAN: I haven't seen the United States Attorney put his elbow on that thing and lean on it as though it was a leaning post and I wouldn't permit them to do it or you.

WILLIAM KUNSTLER: Perhaps I am tired, your Honor. What is wrong about leaning on it?

JUDGE HOFFMAN: If you are tired then let Mr.—

WILLIAM KUNSTLER: Weinglass.

JUDGE HOFFMAN: —Weinglass take over. Maybe I am tired, but I am sitting up here—

WILLIAM KUNSTLER: You are sitting in a comfortable chair.

JUDGE HOFFMAN: I sit in the place where I should sit.

WILLIAM KUNSTLER: While I am standing up.

JUDGE HOFFMAN: I will not permit you to lean on that.

WILLIAM KUNSTLER: May I place my hands like this, your Honor?

JUDGE HOFFMAN: Yes. Yes. That is not leaning. Since you are tired, we will take a recess and you can go to sleep for the afternoon.

November 26, 1969

Judge Hoffman refused to permit John Sinclair, antiwar activist and founder of the White Panther Party, to come from prison to testify for the defense.

The jury was not present.

WILLIAM KUNSTLER: The law permits, but the defendants have a right to decide what they are going to do now when they have been denied a key witness to the Defense. We would like a recess to discuss that.

JUDGE HOFFMAN: I deny the motion for a recess. I don't take recesses—

DAVE DELLINGER: Aw, Jesus—fascist—

JUDGE HOFFMAN: Who is that man talking, Mr. Marshal?

DAVE DELLINGER: That is Mr. David Dellinger and he is saying that that is an arbitrary denial when you say who is key to our defense. I think that is acting like a fascist court when you make decisions of that kind and deprive us of our witnesses. Because he has already been persecuted in one court, now you are persecuting him and us in another one.

RENNIE DAVIS: Why don't you gag all of us, Judge?

JUDGE HOFFMAN: Who said that?

RENNIE DAVIS: Bobby Seale said that.

The jury returned to the courtroom.

ABBIE HOFFMAN: We are very confused about this. Is the Government going to present our defense as well as our prosecution?

JUDGE HOFFMAN: Have you gotten that—what is the name of that defendant speaking?

ABBIE HOFFMAN: Just Abbie. I don't have a last name, Judge. I lost it.

November 28, 1969

Government Witness Richard Schaller, U.S. Naval Intelligence officer

JUDGE HOFFMAN: Oh, I will let the witness tell whether he knows what an obscenity is. Do you know what an obscenity is?

RICHARD SCHALLER: I think I would, but I am sure counsel and I may have disagreement here and there.

LEONARD WEINGLASS: Mr. Schaller, is it an obscenity for the mayor of a major metropolitan area to advise his police to shoot to kill all arsonists and shoot to maim all looters?

RICHARD SCHULTZ: Objection.

JUDGE HOFFMAN: I sustain the objection.

LEONARD WEINGLASS: Do you consider it an obscenity for the United States government to use napalm in the bombing of civilians in North Vietnam?

RICHARD SCHULTZ: Mr. Weinglass can't be serious in contending that these questions are proper on this recross-examination.

LEONARD WEINGLASS: That is perhaps my most serious question in this trial.

December 4, 1969

Fred Hampton was a Chicago Black Panther leader who acted as liaison between Bobby Seale and the defense. He was a twenty-one-year-old organizer, a former NAACP youth leader, and a top student-athlete at a suburban high school, a person who, Tom Hayden said, "made everybody smile." Early on the morning of December 4, 1970, fourteen Chicago police officers attacked the Panther apartment and fired eighty shots. Hampton, found lying naked in bed, was shot four times, twice in the head. A second Panther was also killed: Mark Clark. The Cook County state's attorney, Edward Hanrahan, declared that the police had shown "good judgment, considerable restraint, [and] professional discipline" in killing Fred Hampton, but

*five months later, a federal grand jury found no basis for the police
story that they had been fired on first.*

*The police killing of Fred Hampton horrified the defendants;
Tom Hayden wrote that, when he first heard the news, "I rolled onto
the floor, head in my hands. Some of the staff members living in the
apartment were already weeping."⁶ Then they went to court.*

The jury was out of the courtroom.

WILLIAM KUNSTLER: The defendants respectfully ask the Court
for an adjournment of trial today because of the murder of
Fred Hampton early this morning by police officers here in Chicago. We ask this for two reasons: One, out of respect for Mr.
Hampton and his dead associate, and two, because the defendants—

JUDGE HOFFMAN: Will you wait just a minute? I have to send a
note to somebody who is on the telephone. [pause] You may
continue.

WILLIAM KUNSTLER: Your Honor, we do it for two reasons:
First, out of respect for Mr. Hampton, who was the chairman of
the Illinois chapter of the Black Panther Party, and his associate, Mr. Clark, but, secondly, because of the emotional reaction
of the defendants to what all of us at the Defense table consider
to be a wanton murder of an associate of many of us. It is our
considered judgment that this raid searching for guns was
staged in order to provoke a shootout and the murder of Mr.
Hampton in particular and any other Black Panther that could
be found in gun sight.

JUDGE HOFFMAN: Why should a thing like that be presented to
me?

WILLIAM KUNSTLER: We are asking for—

JUDGE HOFFMAN: The so-called Black Panthers, whoever they are, an organization that I have no familiarity with except as the name has been mentioned here on occasions during this trial, is not a party to this indictment.

WILLIAM KUNSTLER: You may say nay, but I think most of the country knows that it is an issue in this case. But that is not the point of what my motion is.

JUDGE HOFFMAN: I don't deal with the country. I deal with the courtroom, sir. I hear a case and the evidence that comes from the witness stand and in documentary form as documents are admitted.

WILLIAM KUNSTLER: Mr. Hampton not only cooperated with the defendants in the preparation of our defense, but, as your Honor knows, we moved in this Court before your Honor, which was denied, to have him interview for us Bobby Seale in prison just before the start of this case. He worked with us.

JUDGE HOFFMAN: I deny your motion, sir. I have nothing to do with that organization in this case.

WILLIAM KUNSTLER: But you have to do with our sensibilities just as we have to do with yours.

JUDGE HOFFMAN: I deny your motion. Please call your next witness, gentlemen of the Government.

The government then presented several more witnesses.

This marked the end of the presentation of the government's case.

December 8, 1969

WILLIAM KUNSTLER: Your Honor, the defendants are prepared to argue the motion for acquittal. It is the contention of the defendants that the Government has failed to prove a prima facie case as to a conspiracy to violate any one of these three statutes.

The defendants are accused of a conspiracy to travel in interstate commerce, to use the facilities of interstate travel with an intent to incite a riot and commit acts of violence in connection with or furtherance of such a riot, and to aid and abet persons in committing acts of violence in furtherance thereof.

The Government has failed to establish any acts of the so-called conspiracy which antedate the coming to or being in Chicago in the month of August 1968.

You have mere meetings, all open. These defendants, or some of them, according to the proof submitted in this case, were meeting in Lincoln Park, in Grant Park, speaking to thousands of people.

The Government has proved one thing in the presentation of its evidence. What they have proved is that the government of the United States is out by any means necessary to destroy the First Amendment to the Constitution. Your Honor's judgment of acquittal granting our motion will be, I think, a refreshing breath of air in what is a case which has such onerous possibilities and dangers for the right of free speech in the United States.

THOMAS SCHULTZ: Mr. Kunstler said that the Government had failed to prove an agreement. The meetings in the evidence do establish an agreement. The defendants prior to the convention and during the convention were meeting together, discussing together their plans, what they were going to do.

JUDGE HOFFMAN: The Court must at this time for the purposes of the motion made for a judgment of acquittal consider the evidence most favorable to the Government. The oral motions made by the respective defendants through their attorneys for a judgment of acquittal at the close of the Government's case will be denied. We will expect the Defense to go forward with its evidence.

III.

The Case for the Defense

The seven defendants agreed that their defense should go beyond disputing the acts described in the indictment and present to the jury and the country their understanding of "what was going on in America that motivated us to take a stand in Chicago," as Tom Hayden later wrote.[1] They wanted to argue that the trial was an attempt by the government to divert attention from the war, and they wanted to assert an American "right of resistance."

The defendants disagreed on whether to try to persuade a couple of jurors with deliberate, rational argument and thus end up with a hung jury that would avoid "guilty" verdicts and keep the defendants out of jail and organizing against the war—Hayden's position—or to disrupt, defy, and thus "desanctify" the court for the larger audience outside—the view of the Yippies and of Dave Dellinger. Rennie Davis brokered a compromise by which both antiwar politics and youth-culture theater would be presented—a total of 104 witnesses who together would personify the history of the sixties.

The first witness called by the defense was Edward James Sparling, founder of the Citizens Commission to study the violence around the peace parade in Chicago, that took place on April 27, 1968. William Kunstler urged that the commission's report, "Dissent and Disorder," be admitted as evidence.

Defense staff

WILLIAM KUNSTLER: The reason for that, your Honor, is that the document then came to the attention of these defendants and indicated that the police were brutal in their treatment of demonstrators on April 27, 1968. Whether that is true or not is immaterial. They would then make necessary preparations for medical help and the use of helmets, and the like—and the use of Vaseline for Mace, which the report found was used by the police on demonstrators. The purpose of this, of course, is to show the reason or motivation of the defendants in utilizing certain defense tactics in preparation for the August march. They talked about wearing helmets and the like, which, if taken in one way, might mean they were there for offense instead of defense, but if they were influenced by the report, that would go to their motivation in taking those defensive measures. Therefore, introducing the document not for the truth of it but to show the influence it had on the defendants would be vital for the defense case.

Judge Hoffman ruled against admitting the report.

WILLIAM KUNSTLER: Your Honor, we are not going to be permitted to have this witness introduce the report?

JUDGE HOFFMAN: That is my ruling.

December 11, 1969

Defense Witness Phil Ochs, protest singer/songwriter

Phil Ochs (1940–1976) wrote and sang topical songs about war, civil rights, labor struggles, and other issues of the day. He was best known for "Love Me, I'm a Liberal" and "I Ain't Marchin' Anymore" (both 1965). At the Chicago convention protests, he performed at the "Unbirthday Party for LBJ" at the Chicago Coliseum on Tuesday, August 27.

THOMAS FORAN: Your Honor, may we refer to the defendants by their proper names so we will have a proper identification in the record?

JUDGE HOFFMAN: Yes.

WILLIAM KUNSTLER: I think Mr. Hoffman has dropped his last name.

JUDGE HOFFMAN: What did you say?

WILLIAM KUNSTLER: I think that Mr. Hoffman has dropped his last name as a protest against this Court.

JUDGE HOFFMAN: He will have to do that in law. Here he is indicted as Abbie Hoffman. I know that he said that in court, Mr. Kunstler, but his mere saying of that doesn't deprive him of a last name.

WILLIAM KUNSTLER: I know, but legally, your Honor, there is no requirement that you do have a formal change of name at all. A person can drop his last name.

JUDGE HOFFMAN: That is not an issue here. I do not share your view about that, but I think I will ask you to refer to your clients by their surnames.

WILLIAM KUNSTLER: All right, I will rephrase the question, to change Abbie and Jerry to Abbie Hoffman and Jerry Rubin.

JUDGE HOFFMAN: I note some finger pointing by the defendant Rubin.

LEE WEINER: No.

JUDGE HOFFMAN: Defendant Weiner. I called you by your right name, didn't I, that time?

LEE WEINER: Thank you.

JUDGE HOFFMAN: No more of that, sir.

WILLIAM KUNSTLER: Your Honor, I think the record should also indicate for the last few interchanges, there has been laughter in the court joined in by the Court [*i.e. Judge Hoffman*].

JUDGE HOFFMAN: Laughter has nothing to do with what I was talking about.

WILLIAM KUNSTLER: We have a lot of defendants here who have been accused of laughter.

Q: [*to Phil Ochs*] Now would you stand and sing that song so the jury can hear the song that the audience heard that day?

RICHARD SCHULTZ: If the Court please, this is a trial in the federal district court. It is not a theater. The jury is sequestered. We don't want to take too much time. We don't have to sit and listen to the witness sing a song. Let's get on with the trial.

WILLIAM KUNSTLER: Your Honor, this is definitely an issue in the case. Jerry Rubin has asked for a particular song to be sung.

JUDGE HOFFMAN: And the witness has testified that he sang it.

WILLIAM KUNSTLER: Right. But the point is that there has been testimony in this Court that Jerry Rubin gave an inflammatory speech to a group of people at that audience during that day and this is one of the acts which the Government has laid before this jury. What he asked the witness to sing and what he sang to the audience reflects both on his intent and on the mood of the crowd.

JUDGE HOFFMAN: I sustain the objection.

WILLIAM KUNSTLER: Mr. Ochs, I would then ask you to recite to the jury the words which you sang on that day to the audience.

PHIL OCHS: The words? Okay.

It is always the old to lead us to the wars;
it is always the young to fall.
Now look at all we've won with the saber and the gun.
Tell me, is it worth it all?
Now the labor leaders screaming when they close a
    missile plant; United Fruit screams at the Cuban shore.
Call it peace or call it treason,
call it love or call it reason,
but I ain't marching any more.
No, I ain't marching any more.

Cross-examination

RICHARD SCHULTZ: Now, in your plans for Chicago, did you plan for public fornication in the park?

PHIL OCHS: I didn't.

Q: No, I am talking about your plans. In your discussions with either Rubin or Hoffman, did you plan for public fornication in the park?

A: That might have been a phrase. I mean, no, we did not seriously sit down and plan public fornication in the park.

Q: And at those discussions did you—when I say the word "you" I mean you people who were participating in the discussion— you is used in the plural—did you at the discussion discuss having nude-ins at the beaches on Lake Michigan?

A: I think that was mentioned.

Q: At the same discussions did you discuss body painting?

A: I think that was mentioned.

RICHARD SCHULTZ: He was holding back a laugh. I thought that either I was very homely and he was laughing at me or I said something that was amusing to him. I wanted to know.

WILLIAM KUNSTLER: Mr. Ochs is a very gentle man, Mr. Schultz, and he will not laugh at your face.

Defense Witness Allen Ginsberg, poet

Allen Ginsberg (1926–1997) was a founder of the Beat movement and a world-famous poet who was also a scholar and teacher of Eastern religion. At the Chicago convention protests, he spoke at the Mobe's rally at the Grant Park bandshell on Wednesday, August 28. He was also openly gay—which the prosecution emphasized in its cross-examination. Ginsberg was one of the elders of the movement: forty-two years old in 1968.

LEONARD WEINGLASS: Could you indicate for the Court and jury what the area of your studies consisted of?

ALLEN GINSBERG: Mantra Yoga, meditation exercises, chanting, and sitting quietly, stilling the mind and breathing exercises to calm the body and to calm the mind, but mainly a branch called Mantra Yoga, which is a yoga which involves prayer and chanting.

Allen Ginsberg

Q: Now, calling your attention to the month of February 1968, did you have occasion in that month to meet with Abbie Hoffman?

A: Yeah.

Q: Do you recall what Mr. Hoffman said in the course of that conversation?

A: Yippie—among other things. He said that politics had become theater and magic; that it was the manipulation of imagery through mass media that was confusing and hypnotizing the people in the United States and making them accept a war which they did not really believe in; that people were involved in a lifestyle which was intolerable to the younger folk, which involved brutality and police violence as well as a larger violence in Vietnam, and that ourselves might be able to get together in Chicago and invite teachers to present different ideas of what is wrong with the planet, what we can do to solve the pollution crisis, what we can do to solve the Vietnam War, to present different ideas for making the society more sacred and less commercial, less materialistic, what we could do to uplevel or improve the whole tone of the trap that we all felt ourselves in as the population grew and as politics became more and more violent and chaotic.

Q: Would you explain what your statement was?

A: My statement was that the planet Earth at the present moment was endangered by violence, overpopulation, pollution, ecological destruction brought about by our own greed; that the younger children in America and other countries of the world might not survive the next thirty years, that it was a planetary crisis that had not been recognized by any government of the world. The more selfish elder politicians were not thinking in terms of what their children would need in future generations or even in the generation immediately coming or even for themselves in their own lifetime and were continuing to threaten the planet with violence, with war, with mass murder, with germ warfare. The desire for preservation of the planet and the planet's form, that we do continue to be, to exist on this planet instead of destroy the planet, was manifested to my mind by the great Mantra from India to the preserver God Vishnu whose Mantra is Hare Krishna, and then I chanted the Hare Krishna Mantra for ten minutes to the television cameras and it goes: "Hare Krishna, Hare Krishna, Krishna, Krishna, Hare, Hare; Hare Rama, Hare Rama, Rama, Rama, Hare, Hare."

WILLIAM KUNSTLER: Your Honor, I object to the laughter of the Court [*i.e. Judge Hoffman*]. I think this is a serious presentation of a religious concept.

JUDGE HOFFMAN: I don't understand it. I don't understand it because it was—the language of the United States district court is English.

WILLIAM KUNSTLER: I know, but you don't laugh at all languages.

ALLEN GINSBERG: I would be glad to explain it, sir.

JUDGE HOFFMAN: I didn't laugh. I didn't laugh.

ALLEN GINSBERG: I would be happy to explain it.

JUDGE HOFFMAN: I didn't laugh at all. I wish I could tell you how I feel. Laugh, I didn't even smile.

The government moved for an early recess for lunch, and Judge Hoffman agreed.

December 12, 1969

Allen Ginsberg discussed a meeting on August 24, 1968.

LEONARD WEINGLASS: Did you hear the defendant, Jerry Rubin, say anything at this meeting?

ALLEN GINSBERG: Jerry Rubin said that he didn't think the police would attack the kids who were in the park at night if there were enough kids there, that he didn't think it would be a good thing to fight over the park if the police started fighting with the kids, if the police attacked the kids and tried to drive them out of the park as the police had announced at eleven o'clock, that as far as he was concerned, he wanted to leave the park at nine o'clock and would not encourage anybody to fight and get hurt that evening if the police did physically try to force everybody out of the park. That was on Saturday night, the first night when the people would be in the park.

Q: Did the defendant, Abbie Hoffman, say anything at this meeting?

A: Abbie Hoffman said the park wasn't worth fighting for, that we had on our responsibility invited many thousands of kids to Chicago for a happy festival of life, for an alternative proposition to the festival of death that the politicians were putting on, and that it wasn't right to lead them or encourage them to get into a violent argument with the police over staying in the park overnight. He didn't know, he said he didn't know what to say to those who wanted to stay and fight for what they felt was their liberty, but he wasn't going to encourage anybody to fight, and he was going to leave when forced himself.

Q: Now, do you recall what, if anything, occurred at ten-thirty [at night in Lincoln Park on August 24]?

A: There were several thousand young people gathered, waiting, late at night. It was dark. There were some bonfires burning in trash cans. Everybody was standing around not knowing what to do. There was a sudden burst of lights in the center of the park, and a group of policemen moved in fast to where the bonfires were and kicked over the bonfires.

Q: That what—

A: There was a great deal of consternation and movement and shouting among the crowd in the park, and I turned, surprised, because it was early.

Q: Without relating what you said to another person, Mr. Ginsberg, what did you do at the time you saw the police do this?

A: I started the chant, O-o-m-m-m-m-m-m. O-o-m-m-m-m-m-m.

THOMAS FORAN: All right, we have had a demonstration.

JUDGE HOFFMAN: All right.

THOMAS FORAN: From here on, I object.

JUDGE HOFFMAN: You haven't said that you objected.

THOMAS FORAN: I do after the second one.

JUDGE HOFFMAN: After two of them? I sustain the objection.

LEONARD WEINGLASS: Did you finish your answer?

ALLEN GINSBERG: I am afraid I will be in contempt if I continue to Om.

Ginsberg was asked about events the next day, August 25.

Q: What did you do when you saw the policemen in the center of the crowd?

A: Adrenaline ran through my body. I sat down on a green hillside with a group of younger people that were walking with me at about three-thirty in the afternoon, four o'clock, sat, crossed my legs and began chanting O-o-o-m-m-m, O-o-m-m-m, O-o-m-m-m, O-o-m-m-m. I continued chanting for seven hours.

JUDGE HOFFMAN: I wanted to know what your answer was. Did you say you continued chanting for seven hours?

ALLEN GINSBERG: Seven hours, yes.

The testimony then turned to the night of August 27.

LEONARD WEINGLASS: Now, when you left the Coliseum, where, if anywhere, did you go?

A: The group I was with, Mr. Genet, Mr. Burroughs, and Mr. Seaver, and Terry Southern, all went back to Lincoln Park.

Q: What time did you arrive in the park?

A: Eleven, eleven-thirty.

Q: What was occurring at the park as you got there?

A: There was a great crowd lining the outskirts of the park and a little way into the park on the inner roads, and there was a larger crowd moving in toward the center. We all moved in toward the center and at the center of the park, there was a group of ministers and rabbis who had elevated a great cross about ten foot high in the middle of a circle of people who were sitting around, quietly, listening to the ministers conduct a ceremony.

Q: And when you saw the persons with the cross and the cross being gassed, what if anything did you do?

A: I turned to Burroughs and said, "They have gassed the cross of Christ."

THOMAS FORAN: Objection, if the Court please. I ask that the answer be stricken.

JUDGE HOFFMAN: I sustain the objection.

Next Ginsberg was asked about the march on August 28.

LEONARD WEINGLASS: How were you walking?

ALLEN GINSBERG: Slowly.

Q: Were your arms—

A: Our arms were all linked together and we were carrying flowers.

Q: After you walked several blocks, what occurred?

A: We came to a halt in front of a large guard of armed human beings in uniform who were blocking our way, people with machine guns, jeeps, I believe, police, and what looked to me like soldiers on our side and in front of us.

Q: And what happened at that point?

A: Mr. Dellinger—the march stopped and we waited, not quite knowing what to do. I heard—all along I had heard Dave Dellinger saying, "This is a peaceful march. All those who want to participate in a peaceful march please join our line. All those who are not peaceful, please go away and don't join our line."

WILLIAM KUNSTLER: Your Honor, we asked for five minutes two days ago in front of this jury and you refused to give it to us.

JUDGE HOFFMAN: You will have to cease that disrespectful tone.

WILLIAM KUNSTLER: That is not disrespect, that is an angry tone, your Honor.

JUDGE HOFFMAN: Yes it is, yes it is. I will grant the motion of the Government.

WILLIAM KUNSTLER: You refused us five minutes the other day.

JUDGE HOFFMAN: You are shouting at the Court.

WILLIAM KUNSTLER: Oh, your Honor—

ALLEN GINSBERG: O-o-m-m-m-m-m-m-m.

JUDGE HOFFMAN: Will you step off the witness stand?

WILLIAM KUNSTLER: He was just trying to calm us both down, your Honor.

JUDGE HOFFMAN: Oh, no. I needed no calming down. That will be all.

Cross-examination

THOMAS FORAN: Now when you went out to the Coliseum and you met Abbie Hoffman, you said when you met him you kissed him?

ALLEN GINSBERG: Yes.

Q: Is he an intimate friend of yours?

A: I felt very intimate with him. I saw he was struggling to manifest a beautiful thing, and I felt very good towards him.

Q: And you do consider him an intimate friend of yours?

A: I don't see him that often, but I see him often enough and have worked with him often enough to feel intimate with him, yes.

Q: I call your attention to page thirty-two of that exhibit. Does that have on page thirty-two the poem, "The Night-Apple"?

A: Yes.

Q: When you look at that page, Mr. Ginsberg, does it refresh your recollection of the poem, itself?

A: Yes. I wrote it in 1950. That was nineteen years ago. It still looks good.

Q: After refreshing your recollection, Mr. Ginsberg, could you recite that poem to the jury?

A: Yes.

The Night-Apple.

Last night I dreamed
of one I loved

for seven long years,
but I saw no face,
only the familiar
presence of the body;
sweat skin eyes
feces urine sperm
saliva all one
odor and mortal taste.

Q: Could you explain to the jury what the religious significance of that poem is?

A: If you would take a wet dream as a religious experience, I could. It is a description of a wet dream, sir.

Q: You also wrote a book of poems called *Reality Sandwiches*, didn't you?

A: Yes.

Q: In there, there is a poem called "Love Poem on Theme by Whitman." Would you recite that to the jury?

A: "Love Poem on Theme by Whitman," Walt Whitman being one celebrated bard, national prophet. The poem begins with a quotation of a line by Walt Whitman:

I'll go into the bedroom silently and lie down between the
    bridegroom and the bride
Those bodies fallen from heaven stretched out waiting
    naked and restless
Arms resting over their eyes in the darkness
Bury my face in their shoulders and breasts, breathing
    their skin
And stroke and kiss neck and mouth and make back be
    open and known

Legs raised up, crook'd to receive, cock in the darkness
　　driven tormented and attacking
Roused up from hole to itching head
Bodies locked shuddering naked, hot lips and buttocks
　　screwed into each other
And eyes, eyes glinting and charming, widening into
　　looks and abandon

Q: Would you explain the religious significance of that poem?

A: As part of our nature, we have many loves, many of which are denied, many of which we deny to ourselves. He said that the reclaiming of those loves and the becoming aware of those loves was the only way that this nation could save itself and become a democratic and spiritual republic. Walt Whitman is one of my spiritual teachers and I am following him in this poem, taking off from a line of his own and projecting my own actual unconscious feeling of which I don't have shame, sir, which I feel are basically charming, actually.

JUDGE HOFFMAN: I didn't hear that last word.

ALLEN GINSBERG: Charming.

THOMAS FORAN: I have no further questions.

Foran returned to the government table and said to Richard Schultz in a loud voice, "Goddamned fag."[2]

December 15, 1969

Defense Witness Dick Gregory, comedian and political activist

Dick Gregory (1932–) is a satirist and stand-up comedian whose emphasis on black themes transformed comedy starting in 1962. As the sixties developed, he devoted more of his time to political and antiwar activism. In 1966 he ran for mayor of Chicago against Richard J. Daley, and then ran for president in 1968 as a write-in candidate for the Freedom and Peace Party and received 1.5 million votes. At the Chicago convention protest he spoke at the Mobe's rally at the Grant Park bandshell on Wednesday, August 28.

WILLIAM KUNSTLER: Did you see Abbie Hoffman?

DICK GREGORY: Yes.

Q: And would you describe to the jury where you saw him and what you saw him do?

A: At Eighteenth Street, lying under or directly in front of what I believe to have been a tank.

JUDGE HOFFMAN [*out of the presence of the jury*]: One of the defendants who we all remember, I think—he is no longer here—charged me with being a racist with absolutely no basis in fact.

WILLIAM KUNSTLER: He said if your Honor didn't permit him to act as his own attorney you were—

JUDGE HOFFMAN: I would want this very nice witness [*Dick Gregory*] to know that I am not, that he has made me laugh often and heartily.

WILLIAM KUNSTLER: Your Honor, white people have always laughed at black people for a long time as entertainers.

JUDGE HOFFMAN: I want him to know I was the first judge in the North to enter a decree desegregating schools. But that is beside the point. There is no issue of racism in this case.

Cross-Examination

Q: You said he had his finger up in the air. What was he doing?
A: Like this [*indicating*].
Q: His middle finger stuck up in the air?
A: Yes.

Later that day.

WILLIAM KUNSTLER: Your Honor, what is happening? The marshals are taking people out.

A SPECTATOR: Why don't you clear the whole courtroom?

JUDGE HOFFMAN: Will you—

DAVE DELLINGER: You see, we are interested in the truth and you are not and the Government is not and that is what the conflict is here.

RICHARD SCHULTZ: Your Honor, this tactic of one jumping up and then the other, this disruption that is slowly escalating is becoming quite evident and I would ask your Honor to order these—

ABBIE HOFFMAN: Why don't you call out the National Guard?

December 16, 1969

Defense Witness Linda Morse, Fifth Avenue Peace Parade Committee

Linda Morse was a former pacifist and antiwar organizer who conceded she now was preparing for violent revolution. Some considered her frank statements to be a disaster for the defense, but others thought she did an impressive job at explaining what many of the defendants meant by "revolution." Most of this testimony came out in a gleeful cross-examination by Richard Schultz.

LINDA MORSE: The government of the United States has lost its credibility today; there is fighting in the United States today going on in cities in this country today. People's Park in Berkeley, the policemen shot at us when people were unarmed, were fighting, if you wish, with rocks, the policemen used double-load buckshot and rifles, and pistols against unarmed demonstrators. That is fighting. OK? There is fighting going on in the United States right now. People are fighting to regain their liberty, fighting to regain their freedom, fighting for a totally different society, people in the black community, people in the Puerto Rican community, people in the Mexican-American community, and people in the white communities. They are fighting by political means as well as defending themselves.

RICHARD SCHULTZ: Your Honor, that is not an answer to my question.

WILLIAM KUNSTLER: Your Honor, they are intensely political questions and she is trying to give a political answer to a political question.

JUDGE HOFFMAN: This is not a political case as far as I am concerned.

WILLIAM KUNSTLER: Well, your Honor, as far as some of the rest of us are concerned, it is quite a political case.

JUDGE HOFFMAN: It is a criminal case. There is an indictment here. I have the indictment right up here. I can't go into politics here in this Court.

WILLIAM KUNSTLER: Your Honor, Jesus was accused criminally, too, and we understand really that was not truly a criminal case in the sense that it is just an ordinary—

JUDGE HOFFMAN: I didn't live at that time. I don't know. Some people think I go back that far, but I really didn't.

WILLIAM KUNSTLER: Well, I was assuming your Honor had read of the incident.

RICHARD SCHULTZ: [*to Linda Morse*] The more you realize our system is sick, the more you want to tear it limb to limb, isn't that right?

LINDA MORSE: The more that I see the horrors that are perpetrated by this government, the more that I read about things like troop trains full of nerve gas traveling across the country where one accident could wipe out thousands and thousands of people, the more that I see things like companies just pouring waste into lakes and into rivers and just destroying them, the more I see things like the oil fields in the ocean off Santa Barbara coast where the Secretary of the Interior and the oil companies got together and agreed to continue producing oil from the offshore oil fields and ruined a whole section of the coast, the more that I see things like an educational system which teaches black people and Puerto Rican people and Mexican-Americans that they are only fit to be domestics and dishwashers, if that, the more I see a system that teaches middle-class whites like me that we are supposed to be technological brains to continue producing CBW [*chemical and biological*] warfare, to continuing working on computers and things like that to learn how to kill people better, to learn how to control people better, yes, the more I want to see that system torn down and replaced by a totally different one—one that cares about people learning; that cares about children being fed breakfast before they go to school; one that cares about people learning real things in school; one that cares about people going to college for free; one that cares about people living adult lives that are responsible, fulfilled adult lives, not just drudgery, day after day going to a job; one that gives people a chance to express themselves artistically and politically and religiously and philosophically. That is the kind of system I want to see in its stead.

WILLIAM KUNSTLER: Miss Morse, I want to read you something from the Declaration of Independence, which I think the Court can take judicial notice of, and then ask you a question about it.

RICHARD SCHULTZ: Objection to reading from the Declaration of Independence.

JUDGE HOFFMAN: I can think of nothing in the cross-examination that makes the Declaration of Independence relevant on redirect examination.

WILLIAM KUNSTLER: But your Honor, the cross-examination went into great lengths on Miss Morse's philosophy of change of government, of change of the way a society exists, and since the Declaration has relevant statements on that, I wanted to read them to her and have her comments on them.

JUDGE HOFFMAN: I will not permit you to read from the Declaration of Independence. I sustain the objection.

WILLIAM KUNSTLER: By the way, how old are you?

LINDA MORSE: Twenty-six years old. Just twenty-six.

December 19, 1969

Defense Witness Dr. Timothy Leary, former Harvard psychology professor and campaigner for LSD

Timothy Leary (1920–1996) became the most prominent advocate of "the psychedelic experience" with his 1964 book of that title. He was dismissed from his teaching position at Harvard in 1963 because of his drug experiments. He coined the slogan "Turn on, tune in, drop out." He did not go to Chicago for the convention protests. Leary was asked about the meeting in January 1968, when the Yippies were founded.

WILLIAM KUNSTLER: Dr. Leary, tell what people said.

TIMOTHY LEARY: Yes. Mr. Hoffman continued to say that we should set up a series of political meetings throughout the country, not just for the coming summer but for the coming years. Mr. Hoffman suggested that we have love-ins or be-ins in which thousands of young people and freedom-loving people throughout the country could get together on Sunday afternoons, listen to music which represented the new point of view, the music of love and peace and harmony, and try to bring about a political change in this country that would be nonviolent in people's minds and in their hearts, and this is the concept of the love-in which Mr. Hoffman was urging upon us and this was the first time that the coming to Chicago was mentioned.

Leary was asked about a meeting in April 1968.

TIMOTHY LEARY: At that time, Jerry Rubin pointed out that Robert Kennedy was still alive, and many of us felt that he represented the aspirations of young people, so we thought we would wait. I remember Mr. Rubin saying, "Let's wait and see what Robert Kennedy comes out with as far as peace is concerned. Let's wait to see if Robert Kennedy does speak to young people, and if Robert Kennedy does seek to represent the peaceful, joyous, erotic feelings of young people."

JUDGE HOFFMAN: "Erotic," did you say?

TIMOTHY LEARY: Erotic.

JUDGE HOFFMAN: E-r-o-t-i-c?

TIMOTHY LEARY: Eros. That means love, your Honor.

JUDGE HOFFMAN: I know; I know. I wanted to be sure I didn't mishear you.

December 22, 1969

Defense Witness Paul Sequeira, photographer for the *Chicago Daily News*

Cross-examination

RICHARD SCHULTZ: Did you hear anybody, any of the demonstrators, shouting "Pig, fascist, S.O.B." and other profanities?

PAUL SEQUEIRA: At this particular time?

Q: At the time you were at the squadron.

A: No, sir, I do not recall.

WILLIAM KUNSTLER: Your Honor, I object to the characterization of "fascist" as a profanity. He has lumped together a lot of things. I don't think "pig" is a profanity. He said "and other profanities."

JUDGE HOFFMAN: He said "S.O.B." and other profanities.

WILLIAM KUNSTLER: No, he said "pig, fascist—"

JUDGE HOFFMAN: "S.O.B. and other profanities."

WILLIAM KUNSTLER: Right, but I am not sure that the word "pig" or the word "fascist" is a profanity.

JUDGE HOFFMAN: Well, I don't know. We went through a long war about—

WILLIAM KUNSTLER: Fascist has a definite meaning.

JUDGE HOFFMAN: To call a man a fascist is a pretty serious thing.

WILLIAM KUNSTLER: But it may be accurate.

JUDGE HOFFMAN: What do you say?

WILLIAM KUNSTLER: But it may be accurate.

RICHARD SCHULTZ: I don't think Mr. Kunstler is very funny. He is trying to be very humorous.

JUDGE HOFFMAN: Oh, he is trying to be humorous? I thought he was making a legal argument.

WILLIAM KUNSTLER: I am making an argument. Mr. Schultz is categorizing it, and I am not going to argue about his feelings.

RICHARD SCHULTZ: Your Honor was obviously referring to having been called a fascist and Mr. Kunstler is saying it might be accurate.

WILLIAM KUNSTLER: I wasn't referring to that at all. I was saying that the word "fascist"—

JUDGE HOFFMAN: Oh, I have been called worse than that. We will take care of that. I am not sure but that the word "fascist" used as it has been used on occasions is not even worse than profanity.

WILLIAM KUNSTLER: Your Honor, it is used in many contexts every day. It is used in the newspaper one way or another. That is what I am referring to.

JUDGE HOFFMAN: Not every day. I read the newspapers every day. I can't remember when I have seen the word "fascist" in the newspapers except in connection with this trial.

WILLIAM KUNSTLER: Then I recommend today's *New York Times* to your Honor.

JUDGE HOFFMAN: What do you say?

WILLIAM KUNSTLER: I call to your Honor's attention today's *New York Times*.

JUDGE HOFFMAN: Am I called a fascist in that paper?

WILLIAM KUNSTLER: No, your Honor. Every time the word "fascist" is used it doesn't necessarily mean Judge Julius Hoffman.

JUDGE HOFFMAN: Well, that is reassuring. That is so reassuring.

December 23, 1969

The defense decided to present only two of the seven defendants as witnesses, and have them speak for the others. Abbie Hoffman came first, questioned by Leonard Weinglass.

LEONARD WEINGLASS: Will you please identify yourself for the record?

ABBIE HOFFMAN: My name is Abbie. I am an orphan of America.

Q: Where do you reside?

A: I live in Woodstock Nation.

Q: Will you tell the Court and jury where it is?

A: Yes. It is a nation of alienated young people. We carry it around with us as a state of mind in the same way the Sioux Indians carried the Sioux nation around with them. It is a nation dedicated to cooperation versus competition, to the idea that people should have better means of exchange than property or money, that there should be some other basis for human interaction. It is a nation dedicated to—

JUDGE HOFFMAN: Excuse me, sir. Read the question to the witness, please.

The question was read by the court reporter.

JUDGE HOFFMAN: Just where it is, that is all.

Abbie Hoffman

ABBIE HOFFMAN: It is in my mind and in the minds of my brothers and sisters. We carry it around with us in the same way that the Sioux Indians carried around the Sioux nation. It does not consist of property or material but, rather, of ideas and certain values, those values being cooperation versus competition, and that we believe in a society—

RICHARD SCHULTZ: This doesn't say where Woodstock Nation, whatever that is, is.

LEONARD WEINGLASS: Your Honor, the witness has identified it as being a state of mind and he has, I think, a right to define that state of mind.

JUDGE HOFFMAN: No, we want the place of residence, if he has one, place of doing business, if you have a business, or both if you desire to tell them both. One address will be sufficient. Nothing about philosophy or India, sir. Just where you live, if you have a place to live. Now you said Woodstock. In what state is Woodstock?

ABBIE HOFFMAN: It is in the state of mind, in the mind of myself and my brothers and sisters. It is a conspiracy.

Q: Can you tell the Court and jury your present age?

A: My age is thirty-three. I am a child of the sixties.

Q: When were you born?

A: Psychologically, 1960.

RICHARD SCHULTZ: Objection if the Court please, I move to strike the answer.

LEONARD WEINGLASS: What is the actual date of your birth?

A: November 30, 1936.

Q: Between the date of your birth November 30, 1936, and May 1, 1960, what if anything occurred in your life?

A: Nothing. I believe it is called an American education.

Weinglass asked about the plans Yippies made to "exorcise the Pentagon" at a demonstration in 1967.

LEONARD WEINGLASS: Now in exorcising the Pentagon, were there any plans for the building to raise up off the ground?

ABBIE HOFFMAN: Yes. When we were arrested they asked us what we were doing. We said it was to measure the Pentagon and we wanted a permit to raise it three hundred feet in the air, and they said "How about ten?" So we said "OK." And they threw us out of the Pentagon and we went back to New York and had a press conference, told them what it was about.

LEONARD WEINGLASS: Your Honor, I am glad to see Mr. Schultz finally concedes that things like levitating the Pentagon building, putting LSD in the water, ten thousand people walking nude on Lake Michigan, a two-hundred-thousand-dollar bribe attempt are all playing around. I am willing to concede that fact, that was all playing around, it was a play idea of the witness, and if he is willing to concede it, we can all go home.

Q: What equipment, if any, did you personally plan to use in the exorcism of the Pentagon?

A: I brought a number of noisemakers—

RICHARD SCHULTZ: Objection if the Court please.

JUDGE HOFFMAN: I sustain the objection.

LEONARD WEINGLASS: Could you tell the Court and the jury what, if anything, you did at the Pentagon at the time of the exorcism.

A: Yes. I passed out a number of noisemakers and brightly colored flags, arranged for the rock group called the Fugs to carry on a kind of religious chanting and singing, passed out various kinds of costumes and hats and things, and we attempted to surround the Pentagon. Actually I was not involved in any kind of leadership role, just me and my wife trying to do it at that time, and at that point I climbed over a fence and got arrested a few times.

Abbie Hoffman was asked about a meeting in New York City in December 1967 to discuss the possibility of protests at the Democratic National Convention the following August.

ABBIE HOFFMAN: Jerry Rubin, I believe, said that it would be a good idea to call it the Festival of Life in contrast to the Convention of Death, and to have it in some kind of public area, like a park or something, in Chicago.

December 29, 1969

Abbie Hoffman testified that, two weeks before the convention, the National Mobilization Committee prepared a lawsuit with the help of the ACLU to sue the city for refusing to grant a permit for a rally in Lincoln Park, thus denying them their rights to freedom of speech and assembly. They held a press conference shortly after appearing in court. In his testimony, Abbie described explaining to the press that they were withdrawing their suit after learning that the judge was a former law partner of Mayor Daley.

ABBIE HOFFMAN: I read a list of Yippie demands that I had written that morning—sort of a Yippie philosophy: "This is a personal statement. There are no spokesmen for the Yippies. We are all our own leaders. We realize this list of demands is inconsistent. They are not really demands. For people to make demands of the Democratic Party is an exercise in wasted wish fulfillment. If we have a demand it is simply and emphatically that they, along with their fellow inmates in the Republican Party, cease to exist. We demand a society built along the alternative community in Lincoln Park, a society based on humanitarian co-operation and equality, a society which allows and promotes the creativity present in all people and especially our youth."

December 30, 1969

LEONARD WEINGLASS: Monday morning [*August 26*], do you recall what you were doing?

ABBIE HOFFMAN: I made a telephone call to David Stahl, deputy mayor of Chicago at his home. I had his home number. I said, "Hi, Dave. How's it going?" I said, "Your police got to be the dumbest—the dumbest and the most brutal in the country," that the decision to drive people out of the park in order to protect the city was about the dumbest military tactic since the Trojans first let the Trojan horse inside the gate and that there was nothing that compared with that stupidity. I again pleaded with him to let people stay in the park the following night. I said there will be more people coming Monday, Tuesday, and subsequently Wednesday night, and they should be allowed to sleep. I said that he ought to intercede with the police department. I said to him that the city officials, in particular his boss, Daley, were totally out of their minds, that I read in the paper the day before that they had two thousand troops surrounding the reservoirs in order to protect against the Yippie plot to dump LSD in the drinking water. I said that there wasn't a kid in the country, never mind a Yippie, who thought that such a thing could be done, that why didn't he check with all the scientists at the University of Chicago—he owned them all. He said that he knew it couldn't be done, but they weren't taking any chances anyway.

Abbie Hoffman later described his arrest at breakfast on Wednesday, August 28.

They grabbed me by the jacket and pulled me across the bacon and eggs and Anita over the table, threw me on the floor and out the door and threw me against the car, and they handcuffed me. I was just eating the bacon and going, "Oink, oink."

Q: Did they tell you why you were arrested?

A: They said they arrested me because I had the word "fuck" on my forehead. They called it an "obscenary." I had put it on with this magic marker before we left the house.

Q: And why did you do that?

A: A couple of reasons. One was that I was tired of seeing my picture in the paper and having newsmen come around, and I know if you got that word, they aren't going to print your picture in the paper, and secondly, it sort of summed up my attitude about the whole—what was going on in Chicago. It was a four-letter word for which—I liked that four-letter word. I thought it was kind of holy, actually.

LEONARD WEINGLASS: Prior to coming to Chicago, from April 12, 1968, on to the week of the convention, did you enter into an agreement with David Dellinger, John Froines, Tom Hayden, Jerry Rubin, Lee Weiner, or Rennie Davis to come to the city of Chicago for the purpose of encouraging and promoting violence during the Convention Week?

A: An agreement?

Q: Yes.

A: We couldn't agree on lunch.

December 31, 1969

RICHARD SCHULTZ: You wrote, did you not, that you dismissed the thought of attempting to take over a building right across the street from police headquarters?

ABBIE HOFFMAN: Did you ask me if I had the thoughts or if I wrote I had the thoughts? There is a difference.

RICHARD SCHULTZ: It is a convenient difference, isn't it, Mr. Hoffman?

ABBIE HOFFMAN: I don't know what you mean by that, Mr. Schultz. I have never been on trial for my thoughts before.

January 2, 1970

LEONARD WEINGLASS: Could you explain to the jury and to the Court what you understand by the term "Yippie Myth."

ABBIE HOFFMAN: The term "myth" refers to an attitude, a subjective historical view of what is going on in society. It is a subjective reality; the alliance between what actually happened and between thoughts and wonders and dreams about projections. For example, people's prejudices about what they see, since it is subjective, play a great role. There is a famous experiment in psychology in which a man, a white man in a business suit, stabs a young black man in a film and it is flashed very rapidly. White people, because they have a tendency to be racists, will invariably switch it around so that the young black man has the knife and the one with the business suit on is getting stabbed; that is, the victim in a sense becomes the criminal. The events in Chicago would be a type of myth, a kind of subjective analysis. If there was a conspiracy on the part of the government and city officials, you see, to form violence, they would have to project that on someone else. They would have to call the victims the conspiracy that fostered the violence.

LEONARD WEINGLASS: No further questions.

RICHARD SCHULTZ: I have no questions.

January 6, 1970

Defense Witness Richard Daley, mayor of Chicago

Daley was called as a witness by the defense as part of a bold plan to show that it was Daley and police officials who were really to blame for the violence of the demonstrations. The defense hoped to show that Daley had conspired with police and federal officials to stifle legitimate dissent and respond to peaceful demonstrations with tear gas and police clubs.

WILLIAM KUNSTLER: Now, Mayor Daley, on April 15 [*following the assassination of Martin Luther King*] did you not order your Police Department to shoot to kill and to shoot to maim black people in the City of Chicago?

THOMAS FORAN: I object to the question, on the ground that it is leading, suggesting, immaterial, irrelevant, and clearly improper.

WILLIAM KUNSTLER: Your Honor, I have to ask a leading question in order then to move—

JUDGE HOFFMAN: No, you don't have to. I won't permit you to. Go ahead and ask your next question.

WILLIAM KUNSTLER: Mayor Daley, on the 28th of August, 1968, did you say to Senator Ribicoff—

Richard Daley, mayor of Chicago

THOMAS FORAN: Oh, your Honor, I object.

WILLIAM KUNSTLER: —"Fuck you, you Jew son-of-a-bitch, you lousy mother-fucker, go home"?

THOMAS FORAN: Listen to that, I object to that kind of conduct in a courtroom. Of all of the improper, foolish questions, typical, your Honor, of making up questions that have nothing to do with the lawsuit.

WILLIAM KUNSTLER: That is not a made-up question, your Honor. We can prove that.

THOMAS FORAN: Oh, they can? That is so improper. I ask that counsel be admonished, your Honor.

WILLIAM KUNSTLER: I have the source, your Honor.

JUDGE HOFFMAN: May I suggest to you, sir, that this witness is your witness and you may not ask him any leading questions even of the sort that you proposed—especially, rather, of the sort that I heard just a moment ago.

WILLIAM KUNSTLER: Mayor Daley, in one of your answers to my previous questions, you stated something about your instructions to offer hospitality to people coming to Chicago.

THOMAS FORAN: I object to the form of the question, your Honor, as leading.

WILLIAM KUNSTLER: It's not even a question, your Honor. It's a statement, a predicate for—

JUDGE HOFFMAN: Well, ask the question. Don't summarize the previous evidence. I sustain the objection.

WILLIAM KUNSTLER: In view of what you said, did you consider that the use of nightsticks on the heads of demonstrators was hospitable?

THOMAS FORAN: Objection, your Honor.

JUDGE HOFFMAN: I sustain the objection.

WILLIAM KUNSTLER: Mayor Daley, do you believe that people have the right to demonstrate against the war in Vietnam?

THOMAS FORAN: Your Honor, I object to the form of the question. It's an improper form of a question.

JUDGE HOFFMAN: I sustain the objection to the question.

WILLIAM KUNSTLER: Now, Mayor Daley, you've testified that you were at the Democratic National Convention on Wednesday, August 28, and I questioned you about a statement with reference to Senator Ribicoff. Can you indicate what you did say to Senator Ribicoff on that day?

THOMAS FORAN: Your Honor, I object to the form of the question, and again I ask that counsel be admonished. Those are improper questions under the law of evidence.

JUDGE HOFFMAN: I sustain the objection, and I remind you again and admonish you, Mr. Kunstler, of my order.

WILLIAM KUNSTLER: Your Honor, I have tried to reiterate ten times that in view of the nature of this witness, it is impossible to examine him and get to the truth of anything with these restrictions—

JUDGE HOFFMAN: This witness is no different from any other witness.

WILLIAM KUNSTLER: But, your Honor, that isn't so. He is different from any other witness. He is the mayor of the city—

JUDGE HOFFMAN: The fact that he happens to occupy a high public place—other than that, he is a witness. In this Court he is just a witness.

WILLIAM KUNSTLER: Mayor Daley, have you been familiar at all with the report of President Johnson's commission to investigate the causes of violence at the Democratic National Convention?

THOMAS FORAN: I object, your Honor.

JUDGE HOFFMAN: I sustain the objection.

In the absence of the jury.

WILLIAM KUNSTLER: In view of the Court's ruling refusing to declare Mayor Daley a hostile witness, defendants are unable to cross-examine him adequately. [*If the defense had succeeded in getting the court to declare the mayor a "hostile witness," Kunstler would have been permitted to question him more aggressively.*] Had the mayor been designated a hostile witness, the defendants would have offered proof through his testimony to show the following:

One: That there was a conspiracy, overt or tacit, between Mayor Daley and the Democratic administration of Lyndon B.

Johnson to prevent or crush any significant demonstrations against war, poverty, imperialism, and racism, and in support of alternative cultures at the 1968 Democratic National Convention.

Two: That the members of this conspiracy planned and executed the use of every means at their disposal, including the open and blatant encouragement of violence toward demonstrators by police and other military forces, and the employment of savage, brutal, and inhuman tactics to intimidate, deter, or prevent the exercise by the people of their most fundamental constitutional rights.

Three: That in so doing the conspirators were determined to continue the fraudulent myth that the people of the United States had a real voice in their government and that they would have a significant choice in the national election of 1968.

Four: That Mayor Daley obtained and maintains in power in Chicago by the creation and maintenance of a corrupt political machine.

Five: That this political machine by its control or influence over national, state, and local legislatures, the judiciary, and executive offices at every level of government, is determined, whatever the cost, to, through democratic and representative government, prevent the exploration, determination, and effectuation of meaningful solution[s] to the awesome problems presently facing the people of the United States and those of the rest of the world.

Six: That the conspirators, in order to continue and even accelerate their oppressive and inhuman policies, have embarked on a program of intense and brutal repression against all those who are seeking such solution[s].

Seven: That in furtherance of this conspiracy, Mayor Daley among other things:

(a) On April 15, 1968, ordered his police to respond to the assassination of Dr. Martin Luther King Jr. with orders to shoot to kill arsonists and shoot to maim or cripple looters in the black community;

(b) attempted first to obstruct the peace parade of the Chicago Peace Council on April 27, 1968, and then brutalized the marchers therein as a warning to peace demonstrators to stay away from the Democratic National Convention;

(c) attempted first to obstruct the demonstrations at the Democratic National Convention in August of 1968 and then harassed, victimized, and brutalized the participants therein; and

(d) attempted to mislead the people of Chicago and the United States as to the nature and cause of such obstructive and brutal tactics.

Eight: That in furtherance of this conspiracy, Mayor Daley utilized the services of members of his political machine, including those of Thomas Foran, the United States Attorney for the Eastern District of Illinois and a former assistant corporation counsel of the City of Chicago.

Nine: That the indictment in this case was procured as a result of the said conspiracy in order to

(a) shift the deserved blame for the disorders surrounding the Democratic Convention from the real conspirators or some of them to deliberately selected individuals symbolizing various categories and degrees of dissent from American foreign and domestic policies;

(b) punish those individuals for their role in leading and articulating such dissents, and

(c) deter others from supporting or expressing such dissent in the future.

Fourteen: That behind the mayor are powerful corporate interests who determine broad public policy in Chicago but are responsible to no elected or public body.

VOICE: RIGHT ON!

WILLIAM KUNSTLER: This is our offer of proof. This is what we would have hoped to have proved had we been able to have the mayor declared, as we think he ought to be, a hostile witness.

JUDGE HOFFMAN: Your offer is made a part of the record, sir.

WILLIAM KUNSTLER: With that, your Honor, we have no further questions because of the reasons I have indicated.

Defense Witness Ed Sanders, leader of the rock group the Fugs

Ed Sanders (1939–) is a poet, singer, writer, and activist in political and environmental causes who served as a bridge between the Beat and hippie generations. The Fugs, founded in 1965, was a satirical band that sang about sex, drugs, and war at antiwar rallies, including the Chicago convention protests.

LEONARD WEINGLASS: Mr. Sanders, could you indicate to the Court and to the jury what your present occupation is?

ED SANDERS: I am a poet, songwriter, leader of a rock and roll band, publisher, editor, recording artist, peace-creep—

RICHARD SCHULTZ: What was the last one, please? I didn't hear the last one.

JUDGE HOFFMAN: Miss Reporter, read the last words of the witness. I think there were two words and they were hyphenated.

Record read by the court reporter.

Ed Sanders

JUDGE HOFFMAN: Peace-creep?

ED SANDERS: Yes, sir.

JUDGE HOFFMAN: Will you please spell it for the reporter?

ED SANDERS: P-e-a-c-e, hyphen, c-r-e-e-p.

JUDGE HOFFMAN: Peace-creep, Mr. Schultz.

ED SANDERS: And yodeler.

LEONARD WEINGLASS: Now in connection with your yodeling activities—

RICHARD SCHULTZ: Your Honor, this is all very entertaining but it is a waste of time. We don't have to do anything in connection with his yodeling to get to the issues in this case. I ask you to ask Mr. Weinglass to stop making this a funny thing which will last much longer and to get to the issues. If he will testify as to what he knows—

JUDGE HOFFMAN: Beyond mere lasting longer, I will let you ask a question. I am obligated to let him ask a question.

WILLIAM KUNSTLER: Your Honor, I would like to know why we are having people removed from the courtroom again. We were promised an explanation yesterday by your Honor from the marshals, or two days ago.

JUDGE HOFFMAN: You just leave the management of the courtroom to the managers of the courtroom.

WILLIAM KUNSTLER: We can't do that, your Honor. This is a public trial. We have a right when people with beards and long hair are thrown out to know why and we want to know why.

JUDGE HOFFMAN: If you will excuse me, sir—

WILLIAM KUNSTLER: No. I am arguing. I am making an argument.

JUDGE HOFFMAN: You won't excuse me? Then I won't hear you.

WILLIAM KUNSTLER: Your Honor, you have told me forty times never to interrupt you and we have refrained from this. Now you are interrupting me.

JUDGE HOFFMAN: Yes, and I will continue to do so when you say things you are not entitled to say.

January 13, 1970

Defense Witness Julian Bond, civil rights activist and member of the Georgia House of Representatives

Julian Bond (1940–) was one of the founders of SNCC, the Student Nonviolent Coordinating Committee, in 1960, and a pioneer of direct-action protest in the heartland of segregation. In 1965 he was elected to the Georgia House of Representatives, but the members refused to seat him because of his opposition to the Vietnam War. In 1966 the Supreme Court ruled in his favor and he joined the legislature.

WILLIAM KUNSTLER: [*Regarding a meeting with Tom Hayden in a Nashville, Tennessee, motel early in 1968*] Would you describe that conversation, what Mr. Hayden said and what you did?

JULIAN BOND: He mentioned he was interested in demonstrations at the Democratic National Convention, which was then some months away, and as we were speaking, this was the day after the murder of Martin Luther King. As we were speaking there was gunfire and sirens, police sirens in the streets of the city of Nashville. Looking out the window you could see flashes from what we assumed to be guns. An extremely tense situation. The city was cordoned off into sections, the black neighborhoods had been segregated by the police in the city. Tom said that he was afraid that the same sort of thing might happen in the city of Chicago. He was afraid that police violence in this city might occur in the city of Chicago during the Democratic National Convention and expressed time and time again his fear that such violence might result.

Q: At that time did you have any conversation with Dave Dellinger?

A: Well, he talked generally about trying to get permission to march in the streets of the city of Chicago. He talked about marshals, and he had marched then in the funeral procession of Dr. Martin Luther King. This was the day of the funeral, which took place on the campus about a block from my father's home, and I recall him remarking that this crowd, a large crowd of people, had been peaceful, had been orderly, and he expressed his hope that similar crowds in Chicago could behave in the same manner.

January 14, 1970

JUDGE HOFFMAN: Mr. Marshal, I am not here to be laughed at by these defendants, particularly Mr. Rubin.

THE MARSHAL: Mr. Dellinger, also, will you refrain from laughing?

DAVE DELLINGER: That is a lie. And it wasn't Mr. Rubin. We laugh enough and you can catch us when we do but you just happened to get that one wrong. If you can make an honest mistake, that's all right, but to lie about it afterwards and say you saw me talking when you didn't, that is different.

JUDGE HOFFMAN: Will you ask that man to sit down.

DAVE DELLINGER: You will go down in infamy in history for your obvious lies in this courtroom of which that is only the most recent one.

JUDGE HOFFMAN: I have never sat in fifty years through a trial where a party to a lawsuit called the judge a liar.

DAVE DELLINGER: Maybe they were afraid to go to jail rather than tell the truth, but I would rather go to jail for however long you send me than to let you get away with that kind of thing and people not realize what you are doing.

JUDGE HOFFMAN: Now, Mr. Weineruss—Weinglass.

LEONARD WEINGLASS: Weinglass, your Honor.

JUDGE HOFFMAN: Whatever your name is. Continue with the

examination of this witness. Mr. Weinglass. Somebody held up the name [on a placard].

WILLIAM KUNSTLER: We have the name here, your Honor.

January 15, 1970

Defense Witness Arlo Guthrie, folk singer

Arlo Guthrie (1947–), son of Woody Guthrie, sings protest and topical songs about injustice. His most famous song is "Alice's Restaurant," eighteen minutes long, a hilarious protest against the Vietnam War draft. The song tells the true story of how Guthrie was rejected for the draft as unfit because he had a criminal record—a conviction for littering. In 1969 Arlo starred in a movie based on the song.

ARLO GUTHRIE: Anyway, I finally came to see the very last person in the induction center who had asked me if I had ever been arrested. I told him yes, I was. He said, "What for?" I said. "Littering," and he said, "Did you ever go to court?" and I said, yes, and I was unacceptable to the draft because I had been a litterbug in Stockbridge, Massachusetts. The end of the song [*"Alice's Restaurant"*] is the chorus which goes: [*sings*] "You can get anything you want—"

JUDGE HOFFMAN: Oh, no, no. No. I am sorry.

WILLIAM KUNSTLER: Your Honor, that's what he sang for the defendants.

JUDGE HOFFMAN: I don't want the theater owner where this picture was shown to sue me.

WILLIAM KUNSTLER: We'll represent you, your Honor.

JUDGE HOFFMAN: No singing. No singing. No singing, sir.

January 16, 1970

Defense Witness Paul Krassner, editor of *The Realist* magazine

Paul Krassner (1932–) founded one of the first underground publications, The Realist, *featuring withering political satire, in 1958. He was one of the founders of the Yippies and one of the key planners of the Yippie events at the Chicago convention.*

PAUL KRASSNER: I said that Yippie, coming from the Youth International Party, that these were not just coincidental letters, that the word "Youth" represented the kind of generational struggle that was going on in America now. The word "International" because it's happening all over the world, from Japan to France to Germany to Czechoslovakia to Mexico, and "Party" because if this was our alternative party—was a double—deliberately intended as a double meaning, to take off on the Democratic Party and also a party in our sense of the word which was the way it should be, with ice cream and balloons, and that whole thing, that whole going back to the values of childhood, and that the fact that Robert Kennedy had entered the race at this point, I said that he had—he had said that he hesitated entering because he didn't want to divide the Democratic Party, and I said that human life was more important than the Democratic Party and the Republican Party put together, and then I said that—then I announced that we were going to go to Chicago to try to get permits for our festival.

Defense Witness Judy Collins, folk singer

Judy Collins (1939–), one of the key voices of the folk music revival, released her first album in 1961, when she was twenty-two: A Maid of Constant Sorrow. *She helped introduce the songs of Leonard Cohen and Joni Mitchell to the public, and in 1967 she began to write and record her own songs on the album* Wildflowers, *which won a Grammy in 1968. She did not go to Chicago for the convention protests.*

WILLIAM KUNSTLER: Now, Miss Collins, I call your attention to March 17 of 1968 at approximately noontime on that date. Do you know where you were?

JUDY COLLINS: I was at the Americana Hotel in New York City attending a press conference to announce the formation of what we have now come to know of as the Yippie Movement.

Q: Who was present at that press conference?

A: There were a number of people who were singers, entertainers. Jerry Rubin was there, Abbie Hoffman was there. Allen Ginsberg was there, and sang a mantra.

Q: Now what did you do at that press conference?

A: Well—[*sings*] "Where have all the flowers—"

JUDGE HOFFMAN: Just a minute, young lady.

JUDY COLLINS: [*sings*] "Where have all the flowers gone?"

DEPUTY MARSHAL JOHN J. GRACIOUS: I'm sorry. The Judge would like to speak to you.

JUDGE HOFFMAN: We don't allow any singing in this Court. I'm sorry.

WILLIAM KUNSTLER: This song is not an entertainment, your Honor. This is a song of peace, and what happens to young men and women during wartime.

Marshal closing Judy Collins mouth as she tries to sing "Where Have All The Flowers Gone"

Judy Collins

JUDGE HOFFMAN: I forbid her from singing during the trial. I will not permit singing in this courtroom.

WILLIAM KUNSTLER: Why not, your Honor? What's wrong about singing?

THOMAS FORAN: I protest Mr. Kunstler constantly failing to advise his witnesses of what proper decorum is, and I object to it on behalf of the Government.

JUDGE HOFFMAN: I sustain the objection.

WILLIAM KUNSTLER: What did you say at the press conference?

JUDY COLLINS: I said a great deal. I said at the press conference that I want to see a celebration of life, not of destruction. I said that I personally, as a singer, which is, by the way, my profession, as your profession is a lawyer, sir, that my soul and my profession and my life have become part of a movement toward hopefully removing the causes for death, the causes for war, the causes for the prevalence of violence in our society, and in order to make my voice heard, I said that I would indeed come to Chicago and that I would sing. That is what I do, that's my profession.

January 23, 1970

Rennie Davis was the other defendant the group decided to put on the witness stand.

LEONARD WEINGLASS: Do you recall the first time you came to the city of Chicago?
RENNIE DAVIS: The first time I came to the city of Chicago was to visit the International Amphitheatre in a poultry judging contest in 1956. It was the international contest and I had just won the Eastern United States Poultry Judging Contest in 4-H and I came to Chicago to participate at the International Amphitheatre in the contest here.
Q: When you left the last work activity you describe, what did you do then?
A: Since 1967 my primary work and concern has been ending the war in Vietnam. Until the time of this trial I was the national coordinator of the Mobilization to End the War in Vietnam.
Q: Now, directing your attention to the evening of November 20, 1967, do you recall where you were on that night?
A: I was at the University of Chicago. It was a meeting of a group called The Resistance. I was a speaker with Bob Ross and David Harris, who is the husband of Joan Baez.

Rennie Davis

Q: Could you relate now to the Court and jury the words that you spoke, as best you recall, on that particular night?

A: I began by holding up a small steel ball that was green, about the size of a tennis ball, and I said, "This bomb was dropped on a city of one hundred thousand people, a city called Nam Dinh, which is about sixty-five miles south of Hanoi." I said, "It was dropped by an American fighter jet, an F-105," and that when this bomb exploded over Nam Dinh, about six hundred and forty of those round steel balls were spewed into the sky. And I said, "When this ball strikes a building or the ground or slows up in any way, these hammers are released, an explosion occurs which sends out about three hundred steel pellets. Now, one of these balls," I explained, "was roughly three times the power of an old-fashioned hand grenade and with six hundred forty of these bomblets going off, you can throw steel pellets over an area about a thousand yards long, and about two hundred fifty yards wide. Every living thing exposed in that thousand-yard area from this single bomb, ninety percent of every living thing in that area will die," I said, "whether it's a water buffalo or a water buffalo boy." I said that if this bomb were to go off in this room tonight, everyone in the room here would die but as quickly as we could remove the bodies from the room, we could have another discussion about Vietnam. I said, "This bomb would not destroy this lecture podium, it would not damage walls, the ceiling, the floor." I said, "If it is dropped on a city it takes life but leaves institutions. It is the ideal weapon, you see, for the mentality that reasons that life is less precious than property." I said that in 1967, one out of every two bombs dropped on North Vietnam was this weapon. One out of every two. And in 1967 the American government told the American public that in North Vietnam it was only bombing steel and concrete. Then I said, "I went to Vietnam not as a representative of the government, and not as a member of the military, but as an American citizen who was deeply perturbed that we lived in a country where our own government was lying to American people about this war. The American government claimed to be hitting only military targets. Yet what I saw was that pagodas had been gutted, schoolhouses had been razed, population centers had been leveled." Then I said that I am going to the Democratic National Convention because I want the world to know that there are thousands of young people in this country who do not want to see a rigged convention rubber-stamp another four years of Lyndon Johnson's war.

Q: I show you an object marked D-325 for identification and ask, can you identify that object?

A: This was the bomb that I brought back from Vietnam.

THOMAS FORAN: Your Honor, the Government objects to this exhibit for the following reasons. The Vietnamese war, your honor, has nothing whatsoever to do with the charges in this indictment.

JUDGE HOFFMAN: I sustain the objection.

WILLIAM KUNSTLER: Your Honor, at this point I would like to move for a mistrial—

JUDGE HOFFMAN: I deny the motion.

JERRY RUBIN: You haven't heard it yet.

JUDGE HOFFMAN: Oh, there is no ground for a mistrial.

WILLIAM KUNSTLER: But, your Honor—

JUDGE HOFFMAN: I direct the marshal to have this man sit down.

WILLIAM KUNSTLER: Every time I make a motion am I going to be thrown in my seat when I argue it?

DAVE DELLINGER: Force and violence. The judge is inciting a riot by asking the marshal to have him sit down.

MARSHAL JONESON: Will you be quiet, Mr. Dellinger?

DAVE DELLINGER: After such hypocrisy I don't particularly feel like being quiet. I said before the judge was the chief prosecutor, and he's [proved] the point.

JUDGE HOFFMAN: Will you remain quiet?

DAVE DELLINGER: There's no pretense of fairness in this Court. All you're doing is employing force and violence to try to keep me quiet. Just like you gagged Bobby Seale because you couldn't afford to listen to the truth that he was saying to you.

January 24, 1970

Rennie Davis ended his testimony for the defense describing what happened in Grant Park on August 28.

LEONARD WEINGLASS: What were you saying, if anything, on the microphone?

RENNIE DAVIS: I kept directing the marshals to form a line, link arms, and then I constantly urged the people in the crowd to stop throwing things. I said, "You're throwing things at our own people. Move back." As our marshal line grew, I urged our marshal line to now begin to move back and move the demonstrators away from the police.

Q: What were you doing as the police were advancing?

A: Well, as the police advanced, I continued to have my back to the police line, basically concerned that the marshal line not break or move. Then the police formation broke and began to run, and at that time I heard several of the men in the line yell, quite distinctly, "Kill Davis, kill Davis," and they were screaming that and the police moved in on top of me, and I was trapped. The first thing that occurred to me was a very powerful blow to the head that drove me face-first down into the dirt, and then, as I attempted to crawl on my hands and knees, the policemen continued to yell "Kill Davis, kill Davis," and continued to strike me across the neck and ears and back. I guess I must have been hit thirty or forty times in the back and I crawled for maybe—I don't know how many feet, ten feet maybe, and I came to a chain fence, and a policeman fell over the fence, trying to get me, and another police hit the fence with his nightstick, but I had about a second or two in which I could stand and I leaped over a bench and over some people and into the park, and then I proceeded to walk toward the center of the park.

Q: As you walked to the center of the park, what if anything happened?

A: Well, I guess the first thing I was conscious of, I looked down and my tie was just solid blood, and I realized that my shirt was just becoming blood, and someone took my arm and took me to the east side of the bandshell, and I laid down, and there was a man with a white coat who was bent over me.

January 26, 1970

Cross-examination of Rennie Davis

THOMAS FORAN: He [*Deputy Mayor Stahl*] told you there was an eleven P.M. curfew that did not permit sleeping in the parks, did he say that?

RENNIE DAVIS: But in the context at that time it would be waived as it was waived all the time for the Boy Scouts and the National Guard troops.

Q: Well, you didn't consider the Yippies Boy Scouts, did you?

A: Well, I considered that under the Civil Rights Act that American citizens have equal protection of the law, whether Boy Scouts or people with long hair, Mr. Foran. That is a part of this country.

Q: You think that the Yippies with what they were advertising they were going to do in Lincoln Park are the same as the Boy Scouts? Is that what you are saying?

A: Well, as someone who has been very active in the Boy Scouts during all of his young life, I considered—

Tom Hayden and Rennie Davis

Q: Did you ever see the Boy Scouts advertise public fornication, for heaven's sake?

A: The Yippies talked about a Festival of Life and love and—

Q: They also talked about public fornication and about drug use and about nude-ins on the beach? They also talked about that, didn't they?

A: They talked about love, yes, sir.

Q: You and I have a little different feeling about love, I guess, Mr. Davis.

January 27, 1970

THOMAS FORAN: Did you say, "I want to talk about a campaign of building in the United States in 1968 a national liberation front"?

RENNIE DAVIS: Yes. The idea was to build in the—

Q: You didn't say "American"?

A: I said—well, building in the United States a liberation—

Q: —in 1968 a national liberation front?

A: Well, yes, those may be the words, but it is the same idea exactly.

Q: The National Liberation Front in Vietnam is the Vietcong, isn't it?

A: Well, that's your term. Yes. I am an American, sir, and I think that it is time that we began to talk about liberating Americans.

Q: Like the Vietcong are liberating the Vietnamese?

A: Well, I think that anywhere in the world where people are working to—

Q: The same way that the Vietcong are liberating the Vietnamese people?

A: I hardly said that—

Q: I didn't say you said that. I am asking whether that is what you mean; do you mean that you should have a national liberation front in the United States that liberates America the way the National Liberation Front in Vietnam is liberating the Vietnamese people?

A: I hardly think it appropriate that we build an army in the United States.

Q: And what you want to urge young people to do is to revolt, isn't that right?

A: Yes, revolt. That is probably right.

Q: And you have stated, have you not, "that there can be no question by the time that I am through that I have every intention of urging that you revolt, that you join the movement, that you become a part of a growing force for insurrection in the United States." You have said that, haven't you?

A: I was standing right next to Fred Hampton when I said that, and later he was murdered.

Q: You said that, did you not, sir? You stated that, did you not?

A: Side by side with Fred Hampton who was murdered in this city by policemen.

JUDGE HOFFMAN: This trial is going on. Call your next witness. Three of the defendants have gone out.

WILLIAM KUNSTLER: They are bringing him in.

JUDGE HOFFMAN: Oh, it takes three to bring the next witness in?

WILLIAM KUNSTLER: No, but he likes company.

JUDGE HOFFMAN: Does he want to hug the witness too, the way they hugged this witness? I have never presided at a trial where there was so much physical affection demonstrated in the courtroom.

VOICES: RIGHT ON!

JUDGE HOFFMAN: Perhaps that is part of the love-in, I don't know.

WILLIAM KUNSTLER: Maybe this is not a bad place for it to happen, in the United States district court.

Defense Witness Norman Mailer, writer

Norman Mailer (1923–) is and was a leading American writer and author of Armies of the Night, *a book about the 1967 Pentagon demonstration that won the Pulitzer Prize and the National Book Award. He had spoken to the demonstrators at the bandshell in Grant Park on Wednesday. In his speech he said he couldn't join the demonstration because he had a magazine deadline to meet and didn't want to risk arrest. When he appeared on the witness stand, he seemed guilty and embarrassed over what appeared to have been cowardice in the face of the Chicago police.*

WILLIAM KUNSTLER: Did you have a conversation with Jerry Rubin after the Pentagon [demonstration in 1967]?

NORMAN MAILER: Yes I did, in December in my home. Mr. Rubin said that he was at present working full-time on plans to have a youth festival in Chicago in August of 1968 when the Democratic Convention would take place and it was his idea that the presence of a hundred thousand young people in Chicago at a festival with rock bands would so intimidate and terrify the establishment, particularly the Johnson Vietnam War establishment, that Lyndon Johnson would have to be nominated under armed guard. And I said, "Wow." I was overtaken with the audacity of the idea and I said, "It's a beautiful and frightening idea." And Rubin said, "I think that the beauty of it is that the establishment is going to do it all themselves. We won't do a thing. We are just going to be there and they won't be able to take it. They will smash the city themselves. They will provoke all the violence."

RICHARD SCHULTZ: We ask that you only relate conversations pursuant to questions.

JUDGE HOFFMAN: That is right.

RICHARD SCHULTZ: If you are asked about a telephone call, then you can tell about it, but you can't mix them all up.

NORMAN MAILER: You are quite right. I have been exposed to the world as a man possessed of a rambling mind.

RICHARD SCHULTZ: We are to determine facts here.

NORMAN MAILER: Facts are nothing without their nuance, sir.

WILLIAM KUNSTLER: Wednesday the twenty-eighth of August. Do you know where you were?

A: Yes, I was in Grant Park. I felt ashamed of myself for not speaking, and I, therefore, went up to the platform and I asked Mr. Dellinger if I could speak, and he then very happily said, "Yes, of course."

Q: Can you state what you did say?

A: I merely said to the people who were there that I thought they were possessed of beauty, and that I was not going to march with them because I had to write this piece. I just said, "I don't feel right about not marching with all of you because one never knows whether you do this for the best of reasons, or because one is afraid to march. I can't take the chance of getting arrested because I have to write this piece, and so I just came to say, Bless you. Do your business, and I'm with you. Thank you." And they all said, "Write, Baby." That is what they said from the crowd.

JUDGE HOFFMAN: You may relate what you saw, and not what you think is clear.

NORMAN MAILER: I saw the police attack and they charged into the crowd wielding their clubs. They cut through them like sheets of rain, like a sword cutting down grass, and they would cut off a group of people down there on the street and then they would charge into them again and cut them into smaller pieces, cut them again into four, then into eight. They beat them up, left them on the street. Then they would come and pick up more people—in other words, pick up these people who were beaten up and threw them into ambulances. As they did that, they would beat them further. The police kept attacking and attacking. When they had driven people in every direction, they then chased them into the park. They chased them into the barricade that had been set up by the police in front of the Conrad Hilton where people who were just standing there watching the parade were pushed into the police, beaten up. They pushed—as far as I could see, they then pushed people into the wall of the Conrad Hilton. I was not able to see them push people through the plate glass window because that was out of my view.

Q: Could you state if Mr. Rubin didn't use the word "intimidate" what word did he use? What was his language?

A: I use the word "intimidate" because possibly since I am a bully by nature, unlike anyone else in this Court, I tend to think in terms of intimidation, but I don't think Mr. Rubin does. He thinks in terms of cataclysm, of having people become aroused, to reveal their guilt, their own evil. His whole notion was that the innocent presence of one hundred thousand people in Chicago would be intolerable for a man as guilt-ridden as Lyndon Johnson.

January 28, 1970

Defense Witness Ramsey Clark, former attorney general under President Lyndon Johnson

Ramsey Clark (1927–) was the son of a Supreme Court justice. His term as attorney general featured the most far-reaching federal action in support of civil rights in a century, including the Voting Rights Act of 1965 and the Civil Rights Act of 1968. His term also included prosecuting antiwar leader Benjamin Spock for "conspiracy to aid

and abet draft resistance." Clark's term as attorney general ended
when Nixon became president in January 1969.

At the Chicago trial, Clark was prepared to testify that, as long as
he was attorney general, the Justice Department had no plans to pros-
ecute the leaders of the Chicago demonstration. To have the previous
attorney general testifying for the defense in a case brought by his suc-
cessor would have been explosive.

RICHARD SCHULTZ: Your Honor, before the jury comes out, the
Government has a matter which it would like to bring to your
Honor's attention. Former attorney general of the United
States, Ramsey Clark, has been subpoenaed by the Defense. It
is our contention that the attorney general can contribute
nothing to this case. I would have him take the stand out of the
presence of the jury.

WILLIAM KUNSTLER: In a criminal proceeding, where a defendant's liberty is at stake, he has the absolute right to bring
anyone to that stand he wishes, and the only thing that can stop
a person from testifying on that stand is if he, himself, moves
the court to quash his subpoena. Mr. Clark is a friendly witness.
He wants to testify for the Defense. The attorney general's
stand and involvement in this is important to us to get to the
jury. If they never see him and never know, then we will have
been denied fundamental due process of law in that a witness
called by the Defense will have been prevented from taking the
stand.

JUDGE HOFFMAN: The Court is justified in requiring the Defense to demonstrate by voir dire questions of the witness the
testimony it expects to elicit from him. Will you call your witness?

WILLIAM KUNSTLER: Your Honor, we are going to do this under protest. We think it is grossly unconstitutional.

The jury was not in the courtroom when Ramsey Clark took the stand.

WILLIAM KUNSTLER: August 21, 1968, did you make certain recommendations to the President of the United States?

RICHARD SCHULTZ: Objection, your Honor. This falls within security matters.

JUDGE HOFFMAN: I sustain the objection.

WILLIAM KUNSTLER: General Clark, was it your understanding or your intention that the events surrounding the Democratic National Convention were to be investigated without the convening of a grand jury?

RICHARD SCHULTZ: Objection.

JUDGE HOFFMAN: I sustain the objection.

WILLIAM KUNSTLER: I have no further questions, your honor.

RICHARD SCHULTZ: The only way that the attorney general could in any way assist the defendants in this case is to have the prestige of having the attorney general testify as their witness. Now that can't be done. A witness is put on the stand not for his prestige, but for what he can lend evidentiary-wise to the case. The attorney general cannot lend anything to the case for the reasons that I have stated, and we, therefore, object to his testifying in the case.

WILLIAM KUNSTLER: There is relevant testimony here. What we are concerned with here is a crime of intent. Evaluation by the highest law-enforcement officer in the nation at the time of of what was happening in Chicago, whether it was overreacting, whether there was a superabundance of military force in this city, and all of those aspects, certainly goes to the relevance of the indictment against these defendants.

JUDGE HOFFMAN: I sustain the objection of the Government to having the Defense call this witness, Attorney General Clark, before the jury, and I also order both counsel for the Government and the Defense not to refer to this hearing or the subject matter thereof before the jury after the jury is brought in.

The witness was excused.

WILLIAM KUNSTLER: Your Honor, can we have the jury instructed that we had called the attorney general of the United States but that for legal reasons decided by the Court he was not permitted to testify?

JUDGE HOFFMAN: No, that motion will be denied.

WILLIAM KUNSTLER: Your Honor, can't they even know he was here?

JUDGE HOFFMAN: I deny the request.

Thus Judge Hoffman banned testimony by the highest law-enforcement official of the previous administration. The New York Times *declared in an editorial that the ruling was "the ultimate outrage in a trial which has become the shame of American justice."*[3]

January 29, 1970

Defense Witness Bobby Seale, chairman of the Black Panther Party

Seale was called as a defense witness almost three months after his case was separated from the rest of the defendants. He entered the courtroom while the jury was out.

VOICES: Hey, Bobby. RIGHT ON, RIGHT ON!

THE MARSHAL: Sit down, please.

JUDGE HOFFMAN: You are Mr. Bobby Seale.

BOBBY SEALE: Yes.

There was laughter in the courtroom.

VOICE: He doesn't know that yet?

JUDGE HOFFMAN: Do you wish to testify?

BOBBY SEALE: Yes.

JUDGE HOFFMAN: All right.

WILLIAM KUNSTLER: Would you state what is the Black Panther Party for Self Defense?

A: The Black Panther Party—

RICHARD SCHULTZ: Objection.

JUDGE HOFFMAN: I sustain the objection.

RICHARD SCHULTZ: We are not litigating the Black Panther Party.

JUDGE HOFFMAN: I will let my ruling stand.

WILLIAM KUNSTLER: We are litigating the Black Panther Party, your Honor, in this case.

JUDGE HOFFMAN: I will let my ruling stand, sir.

Cross-examination of Bobby Seale

BOBBY SEALE: Revolutionary tactics are broad. I could send three or four people out with a community control [of] the police petition; easily at the same time the community can be occupied by policemen shooting, brutalizing, killing, and what I would tell black people then was don't get up in large numbers because all you're going to do is get a lot of them shot. Go in small groups, threes and fours. You can dissemble the pig police force, as we put it and say it, by circulating the petitions to get enough registered voters to place it on the ballot to vote it out. That's what we mean by being a political party and that's what a political party does, it produces revolutionary tactics on a broad level.

WILLIAM KUNSTLER: What was the name of your party at that time?

A: The Black Panther Party. Prior to that, it was the Black Panther Party for Self Defense, but after about seven months, so many people were mixing up our organization and trying to call it a paramilitary group, which it wasn't, so the central committee of the Black Panther Party took the suggestion of our Minister of Defense, Huey Newton, that we drop the "Self Defense," so people could see we actually have a ten-point basic political program which deals with employment, housing, decent education, fair treatment in the courts, a jury of members of our peers on the jury, and things like this here, and our major political objective was so people could see this and we dropped the "Self Defense," because we wanted a United Nations Plebiscite to be held in the black community to deal with the political aspirations and desires and needs of political, economic, and social injustice that we were subjected to.

January 30, 1970

Defense Witness Staughton Lynd, historian and activist

Staughton Lynd (1929–) was a key movement activist and radical historian who had taught American history at Yale and written the book Intellectual Origins of American Radicalism. *Lynd was*

prepared to argue that some of the events in Chicago '68 were "re-
markably similar" to events in the American Revolution. Tom Hay-
den later wrote that Lynd's testimony "explained most articulately the
basis of our actions in Chicago."⁴ The judge ordered that his testi-
mony be offered while the jury was excused from the courtroom.

LEONARD WEINGLASS: Do you have an expert opinion on the
origins of the right of the American people to protest for redress of grievances and when those channels of conventional
protest are blocked?

STAUGHTON LYND: I have the opinion that the right which is
enumerated in the First Amendment, adopted shortly after the
ratification of the United States Constitution, the right to petition for redress of grievances, had a much broader meaning to
the men who made the American Revolution and who wrote
the United States Constitution than we ordinarily assume.

And what they were doing in this petitionary process prior
to the American Revolution was not asking for the passage of a
particular law, but crying out against what the Declaration of
Independence called a long train of abuses evincing the design
of the attempt to create an absolute despotism.

This is what the petitioning meant to them, and the reason
that I think this concept of petitioning is relevant to the situation before this Court is that it seems to me that the First
Amendment was involved in what happened in Chicago in 1968
in a far broader sense than in its particular senses of the right
to march, the right to use a public park, the right to free speech,
and the right of free press.

It seems to me that the jury might wish to consider the entire process of the demonstration, that which made people

come to Chicago, as a kind of petitioning process in which people who felt that their elected government was no longer responsive to them, felt themselves to be in the same position as the colonists before the American Revolution, and came to Chicago to make one last direct appeal to the men of power who were assembled in the Democratic Convention. I don't see how we can say that the American people have a right to revolution as a last resort against total oppression and say that they lack a right of resistance short of revolution to a partially oppressive situation.

This is a form of intermediate resistance full of precedent from the American Revolution, very much in the American tradition, and it seems to me at least quite appropriate in the circumstances of 1968.

LEONARD WEINGLASS: If the Court please, that completes the offer of proof.

JUDGE HOFFMAN: What is the position of the Government in respect to what has been described here by Mr. Weinglass as an offer of proof?

THOMAS FORAN: The Government objects.

JUDGE HOFFMAN: I sustain the objection. You may go, sir.

Thus the judge ruled that the jury was not allowed to hear the testimony of Staughton Lynd.

Defense Witness the Reverend Jesse Jackson, civil rights activist

Jesse Jackson (1941–) was an organizer for Martin Luther King Jr. and was in Memphis with Martin Luther King when King was assassinated in April 1968.

JESSE JACKSON: I guess what I really wanted to say—I hope I have not been out of order, Judge.

JUDGE HOFFMAN: I didn't hear what you said.

JESSE JACKSON: I said I hope I have not been out of order. I don't quite understand court procedure.

JUDGE HOFFMAN: Well, I don't think I'd make a perfect minister, either. So we're even.

JESSE JACKSON: Okay, Judge. We're going to get along.

Jesse Jackson was asked about a discussion with Rennie Davis.

JESSE JACKSON: I told him I hoped he got the legal permit, but even if he didn't, that it would be consistent with Dr. King's teaching that we then got a moral permit, which, rather than getting permission from the city, if we couldn't get it that way, we'd have to get a commission from our consciences and just have an extralegal demonstration, that probably blacks shouldn't participate, that if blacks got whipped, nobody would pay any attention, it would just be history. But if whites got whipped, it would make good news—that is, it would make the newspapers—we expected the blacks to get killed, so Rennie told me he didn't understand what I was saying. I told him that I thought long-haired whites were the new-style nigger, and if he didn't think they would get whipped, to try it, and we continued the conversation, and then he called me back, I guess, trying to get clarity on what a new-style nigger was, and I felt that the country was in some bind as to being able to absorb people with different kinds of values.

The witness was excused.

LEONARD WEINGLASS: Another spectator was physically carried by the marshals from the courtroom.

JUDGE HOFFMAN: Yes. From what I have observed here, I think

that that sort of thing should have been done before. Mr. Wein-glass, I repeat, I have never seen or heard anything in the many, many years such as occurred during this trial.

February 2, 1970

JUDGE HOFFMAN: [*to the jury*] I must inform you that I have called on the defendants to produce whatever witness they had, and they had none ready to proceed, and they did not indicate that they would rest. Hence, I let the record show in your pres-ence that the defendants have rested. The word "rested" means they have no further evidence to present.

WILLIAM KUNSTLER: We object to that, your Honor. Dr. Ralph Abernathy is on his way from the airport to this courtroom. We want the jury to understand that we do not rest. We are prepared to go ahead. We ask merely a few minutes' recess to bring Dr. Abernathy to the stand.

THOMAS FORAN: Your Honor, may we proceed with the rebut-tal case of the Government?

JUDGE HOFFMAN: Yes, you may.

WILLIAM KUNSTLER: I want to comment on this, your Honor, because I think what you have just said is about the most outra-geous statement I have ever heard from a bench, and I am going to say my piece right now, and you can hold me in con-tempt right now if you wish to. You have violated every princi-ple of fair play when you excluded Ramsey Clark from that witness stand. The *New York Times*, among others, has called it the ultimate outrage in American justice.

VOICES: RIGHT ON!

WILLIAM KUNSTLER: I am outraged to be in this Court before

you. I discovered on Saturday that Ralph Abernathy, who is the chairman of the Mobilization, is in town, and can be here, and because you took the whole day from us on Thursday by listening to this ridiculous argument about whether Ramsey Clark could take that stand in front of the jury, I am trembling because I am so outraged. I haven't been about to get this out before, and I am saying it now, and then I want you to put me in jail if you want to. You can do anything you want with me, if you want to, because I feel disgraced to be here, to say to us on the technicality of my representation that we can't put Ralph Abernathy on the stand. He is the co-chairman of the Mobe. He has relevant testimony. I know that doesn't mean much in this Court when the attorney general of the United States walked out of here with his lips so tight he could hardly breathe, and if you could see the expression on his face, you would know, and his wife informed me he never felt such anger at the United States government as at not being able to testify on that stand.

VOICES: RIGHT ON!

WILLIAM KUNSTLER: I have sat here for four-and-a-half months and watched the objections denied and sustained by your Honor, and I know that this is not a fair trial. I know it in my heart. If I have to lose my license to practice law and if I have to go to jail, I can't think of a better cause to go to jail for and to lose my license for—

A VOICE: RIGHT ON!

WILLIAM KUNSTLER: —than to tell your Honor that you are doing a disservice to the law in saying that we can't have Ralph Abernathy on the stand. You are saying truth will not out because of the technicality of a lawyer's representation. I think there is nothing really more for me to say.

JUDGE HOFFMAN: There is not much more you could say, Mr. Kunstler.

WILLIAM KUNSTLER: I am going to turn back to my seat with the realization that everything I have learned throughout my life has come to naught, that there is no meaning in this Court, and there is no law in this Court.

February 3, 1970

WILLIAM KUNSTLER: Your Honor, when Court closed yesterday the status of Reverend Abernathy was still in doubt. I spoke with Mr. Abernathy where I found him last night in Clarksdale, Mississippi, and he asked me to make the following statement to your Honor about his appearance here and I will give it as he gave it to me:

"I left Chicago yesterday after being informed that the Court had ruled that I could not testify in this case. I left heavy of heart because I had interrupted my overloaded schedule and traveled through sleet and snow to tell what I knew to this jury only to be refused the right to do so because I was sixteen minutes late in getting to the courthouse.

"I cannot close this statement without saying that I have just returned from abroad as an ambassador of goodwill for my country. When I was asked questions about my country's system of justice and equality, I groped for words to explain that both existed. When foreigners said, 'You have no democracy, no justice in America,' I attempted to prove that we did. After my experience yesterday in this Court I can no longer defend my country against such attacks."

This concluded the case for the defense.

IV.

Rebuttal Case for the Government

February 4, 1970

James Riordan, Chicago's deputy chief of police

Riordan was called by the government to testify about the demonstration in Grant Park.

RICHARD SCHULTZ: What if anything did you hear on the bullhorn?

A: I heard this unidentified speaker announce to the group that inasmuch as the march had been stopped, to break up in small groups of fives and tens, and to go over into the Loop [*the downtown business district*] to penetrate into the hotels, the theaters, and stores, and business establishments where the police could not get at them, and disrupt their normal activity, and, if possible, to tie up the traffic in the Loop.

Q: Did you see where [Dave Dellinger] went?

A: He left with the head of the group that were carrying the flags.

DAVE DELLINGER: Oh, bullshit. That is an absolute lie.

JUDGE HOFFMAN: Did you get that, Miss Reporter?

DAVE DELLINGER: Let's argue about what you stand for and what I stand for, but let's not make up things like that.

JUDGE HOFFMAN: All of those remarks were made in the presence of Judge Hoffman and jury by Mr. Dellinger.

WILLIAM KUNSTLER: Sometimes the human spirit can stand so much, and I think Mr. Dellinger reached the end of his.

JUDGE HOFFMAN: I have never heard in more than a half a century of the bar a man using profanity in this Court or in a courtroom.

WILLIAM KUNSTLER: You never sat there as a defendant and heard liars on the stand, your Honor.

RICHARD SCHULTZ: Your Honor, I have no further direct examination.

The jury was excused and left the courtroom.

JUDGE HOFFMAN: Time and again, as the record reveals, the defendant Dave Dellinger has disrupted sessions of this Court with the use of vile and insulting language. I propose to try to end the use of such language if possible. I hereby terminate the bail of the defendant David Dellinger and remand him to the custody of the United States marshal for the remainder of this trial.

WILLIAM KUNSTLER: Your Honor, is there not going to be any argument on this?

JUDGE HOFFMAN: No argument.

Thus Dave Dellinger, the oldest of the defendants, a lifelong pacifist, suffering from various ailments, was taken away to spend the rest of the trial in the Cook County jail.

February 5, 1970

The next morning, Abbie and Jerry appeared in court wearing black judicial robes in open mockery of Judge Hoffman, virtually asking to be sent to jail for contempt. Weinglass and Kunstler argued that bail could be revoked, as Dellinger's had been the day before, only to prevent the accused from fleeing the trial, and that Dellinger had never posed a threat of flight. Judge Hoffman rejected the argument.

WILLIAM KUNSTLER: I think we ought to argue the motion.

JUDGE HOFFMAN: I ask you to sit down and there will be no further argument.

ABBIE HOFFMAN: Your idea of justice is the only obscenity in the room. You *schtunk. Schande vor de goyim*, huh? [*Yiddish for "you stinker—fronting for the gentiles"—the two Hoffmans were both Jewish*]

JUDGE HOFFMAN: Mr. Marshal, will you ask the defendant Hoffman to—

THE MARSHAL: Mr. Hoffman—

ABBIE HOFFMAN: Oh, tell him to stick it up his bowling ball. How is your war stock doing, Julie?

JERRY RUBIN: You are the laughing stock of the world, Julius Hoffman. Every kid in the world hates you, knows what you represent.

February 9, 1970

WILLIAM KUNSTLER: I am glad your Honor is laughing and that no one is being put down for that.

JUDGE HOFFMAN: What did you say?

WILLIAM KUNSTLER: I am glad your Honor is laughing because you know I have always advocated that there is room in the courtroom for a little laughter.

JUDGE HOFFMAN: I am laughing now. I don't promise to laugh the rest of this trial. And I guess I am laughing because of what I was about to say. I am not even certain that you understood the references that were made here by one of the defendants in one of the most ancient languages. I don't think it was a dead language, but the language out of which the language came was a dead language.

WILLIAM KUNSTLER: The Defense would have no objection, your Honor, if you used that language for your charge.

JUDGE HOFFMAN: Referring to who?

WILLIAM KUNSTLER: You mean Mr. Hoffman's Hebraic expressions?

JUDGE HOFFMAN: Yes. Well, if you can call them Hebraic.

WILLIAM KUNSTLER: We would even consent to that, your Honor.

JUDGE HOFFMAN: I would think the authorities would call that Yiddish, wouldn't they? I don't know whether you understand that or not.

WILLIAM KUNSTLER: I understand the intonation of it, your Honor, and then Mr. Hoffman explained it to me later.

JUDGE HOFFMAN: Oh, he translated it?

WILLIAM KUNSTLER: He translated some of it, some of the more esoteric—

JUDGE HOFFMAN: I had the benefit of a not-too-accurate translation in one of the newspapers.

WILLIAM KUNSTLER: *Schtunk* I had heard before. The other expression I had to have translated for me.

V.

Closing Arguments and Jury Instructions

February 10, 1970

Richard Schultz summed up the government's case.

RICHARD SCHULTZ: Ladies and gentlemen of the jury, gentlemen of the Defense: Now the defendants repeatedly state they didn't want violence, they were here for peace, but we have proven through their own statements, we have proven through their own actions that that is not so, that they came here for violence and for riot.

Davis wanted the president to use troops to secure [the] nomination. He wanted to use the violence to precipitate, to precipitate the National Liberation Front in the United States where people would group together in anger against the government and that would be precipitated by a riot.

Hayden wanted to create what he referred to after the Convention, the very day after the Convention, as the first step towards the revolution.

Dellinger said that he wanted to bring the U.S. military machinery to a halt. He referred to the people in Chicago as freedom fighters, and on Thursday, after the violence, that horrible violence, he compared the Americans who were fighting in the streets, compared their actions to the actions of the revolutionaries in Cuba and read a telegram from Cuba. That was the purpose, to precipitate, to solidify, to turn against.

Rubin—Rubin told Norman Mailer, according to Mr. Mailer, their witness, in December of '67 that the presence of one hundred thousand people at the Festival of Life would so terrify the establishment that the Convention would be held under armed guard and the resulting violence by the establishment itself, the resulting violence will be such that the establishment will smash the city, and then he said he was going to devote himself full-time to getting a hundred thousand people here to do just that, to smash the city.

Hoffman stated, right after the convention, in the book that he wrote, five days after, that he wanted to smash this system by any means at his disposal. He intended, as he stated in an interview which was published, which we established on his cross-examination, "He wanted to wreck this fucking society." That's what he said.

They got what they wanted. So while the defendants profess that they came here for nonviolence, their own statements belie that, their own statements contradict that.

Furthermore, they couldn't publicly state they were coming here for violence because people wouldn't come. Just as Mr. Rosen said—Mr. Rosen was the witness who was at the resistance meeting on March 14, 1968, where Hayden spoke.

So they told people, many people, and many groups, that they had planned nonviolent, peaceful activities. They told this to the McCarthy supporters. They told it to Julian Bond. They told it to Dick Gregory. They told it to Jesse Jackson. They attempted to enlist the support of these people, to bring these people both to Chicago and also to have these people think that they were nonviolent.

Rubin. Let's take him first. Rubin was clearly the most active of all the defendants on the streets. He said to about two hundred people that the park belongs to the people. The park belongs to the people. Rubin's from New York. Hoffman's from New York. They are all from out of town. The park belongs to the people; that's their park, and they should not let the pigs push them from the park. Arm themselves, he said. Fight the pigs, break into small groups, wait for instructions from the marshals. Wednesday's the big thing, that they're going to stop the Convention. That's Rubin.

There is Davis next. Let's look at Davis. Davis is much more complicated, much more sophisticated, but with the exact same objects. On July 27, at the Universal Church of Christ, of all places, Davis stated that there will be war in the streets until there's peace in Vietnam. Davis organized the Chicago demonstrations with the other defendants to humiliate the United States government. He now thinks that he can go to the campuses and call for resurrection—excuse me—insurrection and revolution. "Resurrection" certainly wasn't the right word.

Let's look at Abbott Hoffman. Like Rubin, Hoffman got people here with his Festival of Life. He said his reason for coming here was to have a music festival and he and Rubin talked to all of these musicians that I discussed, including Arlo Guthrie, Ed Sanders, Judy Collins, Country Joe McDonald, Peter Seeger—he talked to them and said, "Come on to Chicago and sing. Sing and perform. It's going to be delightful."

Well, Hoffman with Rubin used the Festival of Life for that purpose, to get the people here and then create the confrontation where violence would be precipitated and the Establishment, as they call it, would be weakened or destroyed.

Prior to the convention, Hoffman admitted on cross-examination that he predicted six thousand arrests in Chicago, twenty to thirty people killed, and two thousand to three thousand beatings based on fifty thousand people coming here. Did he tell that to any of the youngsters? Did he tell that to any of the musicians?

Now, let's look at the activities and the planning of Hayden and Dellinger. Their primary role, their primary role, was the Wednesday bandshell. I am going to take them together for that reason.

He and Hayden wrote that throughout the final day of the convention, among other things, they would have disruptions to dramatize their demands. They were going to pin the delegates in the Amphitheatre on their funeral march to the Amphitheatre. They'd have another Pentagon right at the Amphitheatre.

Both Hayden and Dellinger spoke on July 25. Mr. Dellinger was in California addressing a crowd there. Mr. Hayden was in New York.

Now Dellinger was speaking in the evening in San Francisco—in San Diego. Mr. Gilman, the young newsman in his early thirties, testified here near the beginning of this trial. Mr. Gilman heard Dellinger talk about Vietnam and the fighting and the brainwashing of the United States prisoners of war by the American government after they got them from North Vietnam; after being released by Hanoi, the United States was brainwashing prisoners of war.

Then after Dellinger said that, Mr. Gilman related the end of the speech where Dellinger said to the group, "Burn your draft cards. Resist the draft. Violate the laws. Go to jail. Disrupt the United States government in any way you can to stop this insane war." The audience cheered wildly. Then he said, "I will see you in Chicago," with his fist up. It is not a crime to state that, but it tells you, did he come here for a vigil? Did he come here, as they say, for workshops?

February 11, 1970

RICHARD SCHULTZ: Then we have the bandshell. Hayden gets on the microphone, and he says, "Make sure if blood is going to flow, let it flow all over the city. If we're going to be disrupted and violated, let the whole stinking city be disrupted. I'll see you in the streets." All right.

Now let's look briefly at Weiner and Froines. Weiner said they should have some [*Molotov*] cocktails. He said, "They're easy to make. All you need are gasoline, sand, rags, and bottles."

And Froines, who participated in the conversation and who recommended the underground Grant Park garage as the alternative, as the best place, and who said he had four cans of gasoline but didn't know whether he was going to use them or the butyric acid, but who helped in making a determination in how they were going to proceed, aided Weiner and abetted Weiner in that activity, and he, too, is guilty of that charge.

We have shown that these defendants, all seven of them, had a mutual understanding to accomplish the objects of the conspiracy, that they had a common purpose of bringing disruption and inciting violence in this city, and that all seven of them together participated in working together and aiding each other to further these plans.

They wanted the riot, to start a Vietnam in the United States. They are guilty of coming here to incite a riot. They came here and they incited a riot.

Leonard Weinglass began the closing argument for the defense.

LEONARD WEINGLASS: This has been a long and tedious trial for all of us. Words have been exchanged in this courtroom. But I must confess at the outset that it is not easy to follow Dick Schultz whom you have been listening to since yesterday morning. I think Mr. Schultz has exhausted, utilized every shred and piece of evidence that the Government has been able to accumulate against these seven men since they started their investigation apparently on November 20, 1967.

Abbie Hoffman and Rennie Davis signed their names to applications in one case five months before the convention. Abbie flies here three times to meet with city officials. Rennie is here constantly meeting with them. Rennie meets with a sub-Cabinet officer of the Justice Department, Roger Wilkins, and finally meets with the prosecutor, Mr. Thomas Foran, and when they can't get what they want, what do they do, these men who want this quiet violence, they file a lawsuit in this building, in the federal court, compelling the city who won't negotiate with them to come into court. And Rennie Davis puts his statements on the record before Judge Lynch where it is stenographically transcribed.

And all of this the Government would want you to believe these men did while they intended to have violence and a civil disturbance in the city.

I could rest my case on that fact. I think that fact alone is hard enough to digest. I think that fact alone inserts more than reasonable doubt into this case.

Doesn't the Government have the obligation to present before you the whole truth? Why only city officials? Why only policemen, undercover agents, youth officers, and paid informers? In all of this time, couldn't they find in this entire series of events that span more than a week one good, human, decent person to come in here to support the theory that Mr. Schultz has given you in the last day?

Now I am not going to rebut point by point every fact which Mr. Schultz relies on. I won't dispute the testimony of Officer Riggio who came before you and said that Tom Hayden, a man who has traveled in the company of Robert Kennedy and Julian Bond, came to the city to let air out of a police-car tire on Sunday night in the park, and to spit on another officer on a public sidewalk, and this was proof of the fact that he was announcing the beginning of the revolution.

The Government has attempted by bringing in these police officers to recite detail after detail.

Lee Weiner. Not a thing.

John Froines. Frapolly said he was throwing rocks at police cars.

Jerry Rubin was seen throwing a sweater and a small jar of paint.

Tom Hayden—letting air out of a police car and spitting on a police officer on the sidewalk.

Rennie Davis was not seen doing anything except they claim he was on the microphone on two separate occasions urging people to fight the police.

Abbie Hoffman was not seen doing anything of a criminal

nature although they, too, say that he was urging people to do things.

David Dellinger, of course, they claim did nothing in the nature of a criminal act while he was here.

They were a crowd that wanted to go to the Amphitheatre, that wanted to march. They walked past the Hilton. They were pushed back up to the Hilton. They wanted to march, and they weren't permitted to march. They stayed in the streets, and they chanted. But does that fact mean the police should wade into them and beat them and club them? Is that the way we have come to deal in this country with people who adamantly insist on the right to gather together in the streets and to protest?

If the sixties as a decade meant nothing more, the sixties in this country, historically and socially, meant that Americans literally took to the streets, as Tom Hayden said, and Jerry Rubin said, to protest their grievances. They took to the streets. That is what Martin Luther King had done in Selma, Alabama, and that is what has been done ever since.

This last remark was objected to as immaterial and the objection was sustained.

I merely want to indicate to you in finishing that this case is more than just the defense of seven men. While you deliberate this case, history will hold its breath until you determine whether or not this wrong that we have been living with will be righted by a verdict of acquittal for the seven men who are on trial here.

February 12, 1970

William Kunstler concluded the closing argument for the defense.

WILLIAM KUNSTLER: I might reiterate some of what Mr. Weinglass said, that these seven men are important to us as human beings, as clients, but they are not really sitting in the dock here. We are all in the dock because what happens to them happens to all of us.

I might just indicate to you that the so-called outside agitator, which is the term that is used by the prosecution frequently, the outside agitator brought the Freedom Riders throughout the South that led to integrated interstate travel in 1961.

The outside agitator leading the voter registration drives led to the Civil Rights Act of 1966.

The outside agitator led to the Civil Rights Act of 1964 that there shall be no discrimination in public accomodations.

The outside agitators led to the Civil Rights Act of 1968 that there shall not be discrimination in housing.

The outside agitators in St. Augustine, Selma, Jackson, Mississippi, Birmingham, these places that have become so familiar in the last decade, have led to all of the reforms, and there is a reason for it, and the reason is that it takes the man who doesn't make his livelihood in the community, and who isn't afraid of losing his job, or having his house burned, to come in and give courage to people who live in communities which are repressed.

I don't want you to leave for your deliberations without

knowing that agitator has an honest, good connotation whether it be Jesus leaving Nazareth, or Debs leaving Terre Haute, or Susan Anthony, or Dr. King, or George Washington, or Mohandas Gandhi, or Harriet Tubman—they are all outside agitators, all in the interest of social change.

Just some fifty years ago, I think almost exactly, in a criminal-court building here in Chicago, Clarence Darrow said this:

"When a new truth comes upon the earth, or a great idea necessary for mankind is born, where does it come from? Not from the police force, or the prosecuting attorneys, or the judges, or the lawyers or the doctors. Not there. It comes from the despised and the outcasts, and it comes perhaps from jails and prisons. It comes from men who have dared to be rebels and think their thoughts, and their faith has been the faith of rebels."

JUDGE HOFFMAN: Unless you get down to the evidence, I will direct you to discontinue this lecture on history. We are not dealing with history.

WILLIAM KUNSTLER: This is not a lecture, your Honor.

JUDGE HOFFMAN: This is a lecture. It is not a summation of the evidence, which is the function of a final argument in the trial of a jury case. Final argument is intended to help the jury understand the evidence better than they might without a final argument.

WILLIAM KUNSTLER: But to understand the overriding issues as well, your Honor—

JUDGE HOFFMAN: I will not permit any more of those historical references and I direct you to discontinue them, sir.

WILLIAM KUNSTLER: I do so under protest, your Honor.

February 13, 1970

WILLIAM KUNSTLER: We have young people who are depressed and dismayed at what they see about them, who cannot accept the ideals and the dreams and the drives of their parents and their grandparents and who are worried and disturbed and are suffering from a malaise of not understanding where they are going, their country is going, the world is going. These are rough problems, terrible problems, and as has been said by everybody in this country, they are so enormous that they stagger the imagination. But they don't go away by destroying their critics. They don't vanish by sending men to jail. They never did and they never will. To use the problems by attempting to destroy those who protest against them is probably the most indecent thing that we can do. You can crucify a Jesus, you can poison a Socrates, you can hang John Brown or Nathan Hale, you can kill a Che Guevara, you can jail a Eugene Debs or a Bobby Seale. You can assassinate John Kennedy or a Martin Luther King, but the problems remain.

I think if this case does nothing else, perhaps it will bring into focus that again we are in that moment of history when a courtroom becomes the proving ground of whether we do live free or whether we do die free. You are in that position now. It is really your responsibility, I think, to see that men remain able to think, to speak boldly and unafraid, to be masters of their souls, and to live and die free. And perhaps if you do what is right, perhaps Allen Ginsberg will never have to write again as he did in "Howl," "I saw the best minds of my generation destroyed by madness"; perhaps Judy Collins will never have to stand in any courtroom again and say as she did, "When will they ever learn? When will they ever learn?"

Government Attorney Thomas Foran gave the final closing argument.

THOMAS FORAN: The recognition of the truth, which is your job, is a very strange thing. I mean, what has happened to us? Are we going to get conned like that: The bad people are policemen. The bad people are FBI agents. The bad people are people who give their lives to government. The bad people are a kid who goes in the navy. That you're only a good guy if you like the homosexual poetry of Allen Ginsberg. Or you are only a good guy if you think Paul Krassner is funny. We can't let people use our kids like that. We can't let them do it because what they want to do, what they want to do, right there, they want to stand on the rubble of a destroyed system of government, the new leaders in arrogance and uncertainty. That is all.

The vision and ideals that our forefathers had just can't be corrupted by the haters and the violent anarchists. "The future is with the people who will be truthful, pure and loving." You know who said that? Gandhi. Dr. King. "Truthful, pure, loving."

Not liars and obscene haters like those men are.

Can you imagine? You know, the way they name-dropped. Can you imagine—and it is almost blasphemous to say it. They have named St. Matthew and they named Jesus and they named Abraham Lincoln. They named Martin Luther King. They named—they even—can you imagine any of those men or the Reverend Jesse Jackson—or can you imagine those men supporting these men if they—

A SPECTATOR: Yes, I can. I can imagine it because it is true.

JUDGE HOFFMAN: Remove those people, Mr. Marshal.

DAVE DELLINGER: That's my daughter.

A SPECTATOR: I won't listen to any more of these disgusting lies.

DAVE DELLINGER: That's my other daughter. Thank you. Right on. Right on. Don't hit my daughter that way. I saw you. That man hit her on the head for saying the truth in here.

JUDGE HOFFMAN: The marshals will maintain order.

DAVE DELLINGER: Yes, but they don't have to hit thirteen-year-old girls who know that I was close to Martin Luther King.

JUDGE HOFFMAN: Mr. Marshal, have that man sit down.

THOMAS FORAN: You see? You see how it works? "Don't hit her."

DAVE DELLINGER: He did hit her.

A SPECTATOR: They hit him. He did hit her.

THOMAS FORAN: Oh, bunk. "Riots are an intolerable threat to every America." You know who said that? Senator Bob Kennedy said that, who they tried to adopt.

"In a government of law and not of men, no man, no mob, however unruly or boisterous, is entitled to defy the law." Do you know who said that? John Kennedy.

The lights in that Camelot kids believe in needn't go out. The banners can snap in the spring breeze. The parade will never be over if people will remember, and I go back to this quote, what Thomas Jefferson said. "Obedience to the law is the major part of patriotism."

These seven men have been proven guilty beyond any doubt. You people are obligated by your oath to fulfill your obligation without fear, favor, or sympathy. Do your duty.

The jury

February 14, 1970

Judge Hoffman's charge to the jury

JUDGE HOFFMAN: Members of the jury, when a person embarks on a criminal venture of indefinite outlines with other persons, he may be held responsible for the actions taken by his co-conspirators which tend to further the common objectives as he understood them. The Government need not show knowledge of all those acts or of any particular phase of the scheme. It is necessary, however, that the Government prove from all the evidence and beyond a reasonable doubt that each defendant charged with the conspiracy was aware of the common purpose, that each accepted the purpose, made them his own and that each phase of the conspiracy charged in this indictment was within the scope of those criminal purposes.

The law distinguishes between mere advocacy of violence or lawlessness without more, and advocacy of the use of force or of illegality where such advocacy is directed to inciting, promoting, or encouraging lawless actions. Thus, the essential distinction is that those to whom advocacy is addressed must be urged to do something now or in the immediate future rather than merely to believe in something, and the words must advocate concrete action, not merely principles divorced from action.

In determining the guilt or innocence of the defendants or any of them, you must determine whether the words spoken after arriving in Chicago, Illinois, as charged in the indictment, were, one: such as to organize, incite, promote, or encourage a riot; two: were spoken or caused to be spoken to an assemblage of three or more persons having individually or collectively the ability of immediate execution of an act of violence which would result in danger or injury to any other person or his property; and, three: were spoken or caused to be spoken with this specific intent that one or more persons who were part of that assemblage would cause injury or damage to any other person or his property as an immediate result of such words.

I have not intended at any time during this trial, and do not now intend, to express any opinion on any matter of fact. If by chance I have expressed or do express any opinion on any matter of fact, it is your duty to disregard that opinion. In addition, in reaching your verdict you must not in any way be influenced by any possible antagonism you may have toward the defendants or any of them, their dress, hairstyles, speech, reputation, courtroom demeanor or quality, personal philosophy or life style.

You may now retire to the jury room.

The jury was excused to begin deliberations.

VI

Contempt Proceedings

One of the most controversial aspects of the Chicago trial concerned the contempt proceedings. Usually no one is sentenced until the jury announces a "guilty" verdict. But after the jury had retired to begin deliberation, Judge Hoffman immediately announced he was imposing jail sentences for contempt of court on all seven defendants and the two defense lawyers. He spent several hours citing specific examples of their behavior throughout the trial.

JUDGE HOFFMAN: The Court now has the responsibility of dealing appropriately with the contemptuous conduct that has pervaded this trial from the very beginning. Much of the contemptuous conduct in this case does not show, of record. The constant murmurs and snickering emanating from the Defense table were not captured on the printed page. No record, no matter how skillfully transcribed, can adequately portray the venom, sarcasm, and tone of voice employed by a speaker. No record, no matter how skillfully transcribed, can adequately reflect the applause, the guffaws, and other subtle tactics employed by these contemnors in an attempt to break up this trial. I have not focused on these cheap theatrics, histrionics, and affectations. I note them for the record lest my silence be construed as approval.

Judge Hoffman

From the outset of the trial the Court admonished and warned the defendants and their counsel to refrain from such conduct, particularly when committed in the presence of the jury. They chose deliberately to disregard such admonition, right down through yesterday afternoon's hearing, and have openly challenged and flaunted their contempt for both this Court and for the system of law it represents.

WILLIAM KUNSTLER: We place little credence in the notion that the independence of the judiciary hangs on the power to try contempt summarily and are not persuaded that the additional time and expense possibly involved in submitting serious contempts to juries will seriously handicap the effective functioning of the courts. We do not deny that serious punishment must sometimes be imposed for contempt but we reject the contention that such punishment must be imposed without a right to jury trial.

JUDGE HOFFMAN: I will first consider the conduct of the defendant David Dellinger. The Court finds that the defendant Dellinger is guilty of direct contempt of court. The defendant will be committed—by the way, does counsel for Dellinger want to be heard before sentence is imposed?

WILLIAM KUNSTLER: Your Honor, I have a legal argument on the power of the Court after trial. Summary contempt is only a method of preventing disturbance during trial, but after trial a man [accused of contempt] is entitled to a jury trial. Furthermore, Rule 42(b) of the U.S. criminal code says if the contempt charge involved disrespect to or criticism of a judge, that judge is disqualified from presiding at the trial or hearing except with the defendant's consent. The defendants do not consent to your Honor sitting on their contempts and therefore I think your Honor is totally without jurisdiction to do what you are doing today.

JUDGE HOFFMAN: I do not share your view. Mr. Dellinger, do you care to say anything? Only in respect to punishment, I will hear you.

DAVE DELLINGER: You want us to be like good Germans supporting the evils of our decade and then when we refused to be good Germans and came to Chicago and demonstrated, despite the threats and intimidations of the establishment, now you want us to be like good Jews, going quietly and politely to the concentration camps while you and this Court suppress freedom and the truth. And the fact is that I am not prepared to do that. You want us to stay in our place like black people were supposed to stay in their place—

JUDGE HOFFMAN: Mr. Marshal, I will ask you to have Mr. Dellinger sit down.

DAVE DELLINGER: —like poor people were supposed to stay in their place, like people without formal education are supposed to stay in their place, like women are supposed to stay in their place—

JUDGE HOFFMAN: I will ask you to sit down.

DAVE DELLINGER: Like children are supposed to stay in their place, like lawyers—for whom I thank—I thank you—are supposed to stay in their places. People no longer will be quiet. People are going to speak up. I am an old man and I am just speaking feebly and not too well, but I reflect the spirit that will echo—

JUDGE HOFFMAN: Take him out—

DAVE DELLINGER: —throughout the world—

Applause.

DAVE DELLINGER: —comes from my children who came yesterday—

At this point complete disorder broke out in the courtroom. Kunstler burst into tears.

DAVE DELLINGER: Leave my daughters alone. Leave my daughters alone.

WILLIAM KUNSTLER: My life has come to nothing, I am not anything anymore. You destroyed me and everybody else. Put me in jail now, for God's sakes, and get me out of this place. Come to mine now. Come to mine now. Judge, please. Please. I beg you. Come to mine. Do me, too, I don't want to be out.

Dave Dellinger was then sentenced by Judge Hoffman to twenty-nine months and sixteen days on thirty-two counts of contempt.

RENNIE DAVIS: You have just jailed one of the most beautiful and one of the most courageous men in the United States.

JUDGE HOFFMAN: All right. Now we will talk about you, Mr. Davis.

RENNIE DAVIS: Judge, you represent all that is old, ugly, bigoted and repressive in this country, and I will tell you that the spirit at this Defense table is going to devour your sickness in the next generation.

Rennie Davis was sentenced to twenty-five months and fourteen days on twenty-three counts of contempt.

JUDGE HOFFMAN: We now come to the consideration of the matter of Thomas Hayden.

TOM HAYDEN: Your Honor, before your eyes you see the most vital ingredient of your system collapsing because the system does not hold together.

JUDGE HOFFMAN: Oh, don't be so pessimistic. Our system isn't collapsing. Fellows as smart as you could do awfully well under this system. I am not trying to convert you, mind you.

ABBIE HOFFMAN: We don't want a place in the regiment, Julie.

TOM HAYDEN: I was trying to think about what I regretted and about punishment. I can only state one thing that affected my feelings, my own feelings, and that is that I would like to have a child.

JUDGE HOFFMAN: There is where the federal system can do you no good.

TOM HAYDEN: The federal system can do you no good in trying to prevent the birth of a new world.

Tom Hayden was sentenced to fourteen months and fourteen days on eleven counts of contempt.

JUDGE HOFFMAN: I will hear from Mr. Hoffman if he wants to be heard.

ABBIE HOFFMAN: You said that we did not pay tribute to the highest court in the land, but to us the federal court is not the highest court in the land.

JUDGE HOFFMAN: I didn't hear myself say that.

ABBIE HOFFMAN: Oh, yes, you did. You always call it the highest court in the land. Sure.

JUDGE HOFFMAN: The Supreme Court is.

ABBIE HOFFMAN: We don't consider it the highest. We consider the people the highest court in the land.

We cannot respect an authority that we regard as illegitimate. We can only offer resistance to such illegitimate authority.

We cannot respect a law that is tyranny and the courts are in a conspiracy of tyranny. And when the law is in tyranny, the only order is insurrection and disrespect, and that's what we showed, and that's what all honorable men of free will will show.

Abbie Hoffman was sentenced to eight months on twenty-four counts of contempt.

February 15, 1970

JUDGE HOFFMAN: I come now to deal with the conduct of Jerry Rubin during this trial. I will hear Mr. Rubin if he desires to be heard.

JERRY RUBIN: I want to discuss the contempts and the motivation behind them, which would affect your punishment and I want to start with the references that I have made on a number of occasions to [the] Gestapo, fascism, and Hitler, and I want to explain what motivated me to say that.

Everything that happened in Nazi Germany was legal. It happened in courtrooms, just like this. It was done by judges, judges who wore robes and judges who quoted the law and judges who said, "This is the law, respect it."

Just quoting the law is no answer, because the law in the courtroom gagged and chained Bobby Seale and I refuse to stand up and say, "Heil Hitler" when a black man was gagged and chained and I think that any human being sitting in that courtroom refused to stand up and that's why I refused to stand up because I came to this trial. I wanted to be indicted.

By having to punish us, you have shown the world that this judicial system has lost the respect of the youth, and the youth will free us. We're going to jail with smiles on our faces because we know that in jail, there are millions of kids, young kids out there who identify with us, and are going to fight to free us, and that's the revolution. And your jailing us is a vindictive, revengeful act.

JUDGE HOFFMAN: You may sit down.

JERRY RUBIN: I am happy to.

Jerry Rubin was sentenced to twenty-five months and twenty-three days on fifteen counts of contempt.

JUDGE HOFFMAN: We now come to the consideration of the conduct of defendant Lee Weiner. I am supposed to be especially tolerant because years ago when I was a much younger man, I was a member of the faculty of the school that you—I don't know whether you still are; at least it has been suggested here during this trial that you are or were a teacher there.

LEE WEINER: I even understand that there is a plaque naming an auditorium after you at the law school. At latest report, by the way—

JUDGE HOFFMAN: You are nice to tell the assembled spectators here—

LEE WEINER: I tell them actually for an evil reason.

JUDGE HOFFMAN: —that there is a Hoffman Hall on Northwestern University's campus.

LEE WEINER: I am telling them actually because I am suggesting it is evil.

JUDGE HOFFMAN: Perhaps those who think ill of me because of some of the things that have been said might have a little compassion.

LEE WEINER: I am pleased to report to you that the plaque has been ripped off the wall.

JUDGE HOFFMAN: The plaque?

LEE WEINER: The plaque has been ripped off the wall in the auditorium. Apparently while the Board of Trustees feel affection for you, the student body does not.

JUDGE HOFFMAN: Did they take the sign off the door?

LEE WEINER: They have done their best. They have done their best.

Lee Weiner was sentenced to two months and eighteen days on seven counts of contempt.

Lee Weiner using sign
language to his girl friend.

Lee Weiner

JUDGE HOFFMAN: I will next consider the conduct of the lawyers in this case—oh, I beg your pardon. We have—I almost forgot to take care of Mr. Froines.

JOHN FROINES: It's part of being a media unknown that even the Judge finally forgets you're here.

John Froines was sentenced to five months and fifteen days on ten counts of contempt.

JUDGE HOFFMAN: This matter now involves the conduct of Mr. William Kunstler, counsel for some of the defendants here, who has participated in this trial from the very beginning.

WILLIAM KUNSTLER: I just have a few words, your Honor.

Your Honor, I have been a lawyer since December of 1948, when I was first admitted to the bar in the state of New York.

Until today I have never once been disciplined by any judge, federal or state, although a large part of my practice, at least for the last decade, has taken place in hostile Southern courts where I was representing black and white clients in highly controversial civil rights cases.

Yesterday, for the first time in my career, I completely lost my composure in a courtroom, as I watched the older daughter of David Dellinger being rushed out of the room because she clapped her hands to acknowledge what amounted to her father's farewell statement to her.

I felt then such a deep sense of utter futility that I could not help crying, something I had not done publicly since childhood.

I am sorry if I disturbed the decorum of the courtroom, but

John Froines, Judge Hoffman, and Tom Hayden

I am not ashamed of my conduct in this Court, for which I am about to be punished.

But to those lawyers who may, in learning of what may happen to me, waver, I can only say this: Stand firm, remain true to those ideals of the law which even if openly violated here and in other places, are true and glorious goals, and, above all, never desert those principles of equality, justice, and freedom without which life has little if any meaning.

I may not be the greatest lawyer in the world, your Honor, but I think that I am at this moment, along with my colleague, Leonard Weinglass, the most privileged. We are being punished for what we believe in.

Your Honor, I am ready, sir, to be sentenced, and I would appreciate it if I could be permitted to remain standing at this lectern where I have spent the greater part of the past five months, while you do so. Thank you.
Applause.

William Kunstler was sentenced to four years and thirteen days on twenty-four counts of contempt.

JUDGE HOFFMAN: Now we come to the matter of Leonard Weinglass.

This trial, whatever the result comes to be, could have been conducted fairly and with dignity and without rancor or ill will. I can recall few instances—oh, I suppose every judge has a run-in with lawyers on occasions, but there have been few instances that I can recall where I have had acrimonious or anything that approached an acrimonious discussion with a lawyer in respect to his conduct. I will hear you now only on the matter—I took time to digress because of your observations about—

LEONARD WEINGLASS: If I could just answer that digression for a moment: With respect to our different understandings of respect, I was hopeful when I came here that after twenty weeks the Court would know my name and I didn't receive that which I thought was the minimum—

JUDGE HOFFMAN: Well, I am going to tell you about that. I have got a very close friend named Weinruss and I know nobody by the name of Weinrob—and somehow or other the name of Weinruss stuck in my mind and it is your first appearance here.

Leonard Weinglass was sentenced to twenty months and nine days on fourteen counts of contempt.

VII.

Verdicts and Sentencing

February 18, 1970

JUDGE HOFFMAN: I understand, gentlemen, that the jury has brought in a verdict. Is the jury here?

THE MARSHAL: Your Honor, the jury has reached a verdict.

Thus, after four days of deliberations, the defense strategy of seeking a hung jury, unable to reach a unanimous verdict, failed.

RICHARD SCHULTZ: Considering what has gone on in this courtroom before, considering the fact that we have had a number of fist fights in the courtroom and miniature riots right here in this courtroom and the last especially culminating last week even during the final arguments with the staff members, relative to the defendants, who have been thrown out repeatedly—some, in fact, are under charge before the United States Commissioner—and further because, your Honor, on Saturday and on Sunday your Honor issued certain contempt citations in this case, we would ask your Honor to have the Court cleared of all spectators except the press.

JUDGE HOFFMAN: You may reply, Mr. Kunstler.

WILLIAM KUNSTLER: Your Honor, we would want to voice the strongest possible objection to the first point, the first application by the Government, that is, that the Court be cleared during the rendering of the verdict. It is our contention—and I think the facts bear it out—that if there was violence in this courtroom, it was provoked in the courtroom by either the Government or the United States marshals involved and that the violence that was provoked was far in excess of any required. I don't think that you ought to add to what we consider a totally unfair trial the last crowning indignity that you could possibly do as far as these defendants were concerned and that is to let them stand here alone surrounded only by the press, by the prosecution, and with their own attorneys, but really alone in the most lonely way a man can be alone, divorced from his family and friends and supporters at a moment in his life when he is about to hear the verdict of a jury in a criminal case and one involving serious criminal penalties.

JUDGE HOFFMAN: I will decide to enter this order: The following may remain: of course the defendants and those who have sat at the Government's table throughout this trial—the three lawyers and representatives of the Government. The defendants. The ladies and gentlemen of the press, all media. I direct that no newspapers be exhibited in the presence of the jury. I would say counsel of record, of course, for the defendants may be here. Now all of the parties here other than those I have mentioned are directed to leave the courtroom.

A VOICE: They will dance on your grave, Julie, and the graves of the pig empire.

JUDGE HOFFMAN: Good morning, ladies and gentlemen of the jury. I am informed by the United States marshal that you have reached a verdict or come to some verdicts.

THE FOREMAN: Yes, your Honor.

JUDGE HOFFMAN: Would you hand the verdicts to the marshal, please, and, Mr. Marshal, will you hand them to the clerk? I direct the clerk to read the verdicts.

Lee Weiner and John Froines were found not guilty on all charges. All seven defendants were found not guilty of conspiracy.

    Dave Dellinger, Rennie Davis, Tom Hayden, Abbie Hoffman, and Jerry Rubin were found guilty of crossing state lines to incite a riot.

JUDGE HOFFMAN: Thank you, ladies and gentlemen. I wish I were eloquent enough to express my appreciation to you for your several months of service in this case, one of the most difficult I ever tried, one of the longest, and I know you had a great responsibility also. You are excused now.

WILLIAM KUNSTLER: I would urge that your Honor continue the bond that is presently in effect, even though they have been convicted on one count of the two, and it was thought sufficient to only have a ten-thousand-dollar bond for that, for the two counts originally, that your Honor continue the bond on appeal, pending appeal of this cause, of the ten-thousand-dollar bond previously established by this Court for the five men I have mentioned.

JUDGE HOFFMAN: I have heard the evidence here. I have watched all of the defendants whom you asked me to release on bail with respect to the counts on which they have been found guilty. From the evidence and from their conduct in this trial, I find they are dangerous men to be at large and I deny your motion for bail as to Dellinger, Davis, Hayden, Hoffman, and Rubin respectively.

February 20, 1970

JUDGE HOFFMAN: I now proceed with the imposition of sentence. I will hear you for your clients, Mr. Kunstler.

WILLIAM KUNSTLER: Your Honor, for all of the defendants, Mr. Weinglass and I are going to make no statement. The defendants will speak for themselves.

JUDGE HOFFMAN: All right. Mr. Dellinger, you have the right to speak in your own behalf.

DAVE DELLINGER: First, I think that every judge should be required to spend time in prison before sentencing other people there so that he might become aware of the degrading antihuman conditions that persist not only in Cook County Jail but in the prisons generally of this country.

I feel more compassion for you, sir, than I do any hostility. I feel that you are a man who has had too much power over the lives of too many people for too many years.

I want to say that sending us to prison, any punishment the government can impose upon us, will not solve the problems that have gotten us into "trouble" with the government and the law in the first place.

Our movement is not very strong today. It is not united, it is not well organized. It is very confused and makes a lot of mistakes, but there is the beginning of an awakening in this country which has been going on for at least the last fifteen years, and it is an awakening that will not be denied. Tactics will change, people will err, people will die in the streets and die in prison, but I do not believe that this movement can be denied because however falsely applied the American ideal was from the beginning when it excluded black people, and Indians, and people without property, nonetheless there was a dream of

Dave Dellinger

justice and equality and freedom, and brotherhood, and I think that that dream is much closer to fulfillment today than it has been at any time in the history of this country.

I only wish that we were all not just more eloquent, I wish we were smarter, more dedicated, more united. I wish we could work together. I wish we could reach out to the Forans, and the Schultzes, and the Hoffmans, and convince them of the necessity of this revolution.

JUDGE HOFFMAN: Mr. Davis, would you like to speak in your own behalf? You have that right.

RENNIE DAVIS: I do not think that it is a time to appeal to you or to appeal to the system that is about to put me away.

I suppose if I were to make any appeals, it really should be to Agent Stanley or to J. Edgar Hoover, because the sentence that I am about to receive comes not from you in my judgment but from the FBI.

I guess if I have any hope at all it is that I am allowed out of prison by 1976 because in 1976 the American people are not going to recount their history, they are going to relive their history, and when I come out of prison it will be to move next door to Tom Foran. I am going to be the boy next door to Tom Foran and the boy next door, the boy that could have been a judge, could have been a prosecutor, could have been a college professor, is going to move next door to organize his kids into the revolution. We are going to turn the sons and daughters of the ruling class in this country into Vietcong.

JUDGE HOFFMAN: Mr. Hayden, you have a right to speak in your own behalf.

Rennie Davis

Tom Hayden

TOM HAYDEN: Our intention in coming to Chicago was not to incite a riot. Our intention in coming to Chicago was to see to it that certain things, that is, the right of every human being, the right to assemble, the right to protest, can be carried out even where the government chooses to suspend those rights. It was because we chose to exercise those rights in Chicago in the jaws of a police state that we are here today.

We would hardly be notorious characters if they had left us alone in the streets of Chicago last year. It would have been a few thousand people. It would have been testimony to our failure as organizers. But instead we became the architects, the masterminds, and the geniuses of a conspiracy to overthrow the government. We were invented. We were chosen by the government to serve as scapegoats for all that they wanted to prevent happening in the 1970s.

It is all right to let Mafia people out on bail. It is all right to let murderers out on bail. They walked right out of the court-room; it is not going to be all right to let us out on bail because they will say, there is an incendiary situation.

If you didn't want to make us martyrs, why did you do it? If you wanted to keep it cool, why didn't you give us a permit? You know. You know if you had given us a permit, you know if you had given slightly different instructions, very little would have happened last year in Chicago. Ramsey Clark knows it. He survived many more street confrontations than most people in this room, no matter how much you want to call him an intel-lectual from Washington.

JUDGE HOFFMAN: Mr. Hoffman, the law gives you the right to speak in your own behalf. I will hear you if you have anything to say.

ABBIE HOFFMAN: Thank you.

Right from the beginning of the indictment, up until the end of the trial, I always wanted to change my plea. I had just like a great urge to confess; say, "I am guilty," because I felt what the State was calling me was an enemy of the State and I am an enemy of the State, I am an enemy of the America as it is now, with a K.

He says we are un-American. I don't feel un-American. I feel very American. I said it is not that the Yippies hate Amer-ica. It is that they feel the American dream has been betrayed. That has been my attitude.

Abbie pointed to the portraits of founding fathers on the wall behind the judge.

I know those guys on the wall. I know them better than you, I feel. I know Adams. I mean, I know all the Adams. They grew up twenty miles from my home in Massachusetts. I played with Sam Adams on the Concord Bridge. I was there when Paul Revere rode right up on his motorcycle and said, "The pigs are coming, the pigs are coming. Right into Lexington." Thomas Jefferson. Thomas Jefferson called for revolution every ten years. Thomas Jefferson had an agrarian reform program that made Mao Tse-tung look like a liberal. I know Thomas Jefferson.

Washington? I now respect Bobby Seale's opinion of him as a slaveholder because he was. All men are children of their times, even revolutionaries. We are children of our times and we are not perfect. Washington grew pot. He called it hemp. It was called hemp then. He was probably a pothead.

Abraham Lincoln? There is another one. In 1861 Abraham Lincoln in his inaugural address said, and I quote, "When the people shall grow weary of their constitutional right to amend the government, they shall exert their revolutionary right to dismember and overthrow that government." He gave that speech. If Abraham Lincoln had given that speech in Lincoln Park, he would be on trial right here, right here in this courtroom, because that is an inciteful speech.

I didn't want to be that serious. I was supposed to be funny. I tried to be, I mean, but it was sad last night.

It wasn't funny last night sitting in a prison cell, a five-by-eight room, with no light in the room.

There's no light. It's not a nice place for a Jewish boy to be, with a college education. I'm sure my mother would say that.

Speaking about that, I remember when we were speaking

Abbie Hoffman

before, you said, "Tom Hayden, you could have had a nice position in the system, you could have had a job in the firm." We
have heard that for the past ten years, all of us have heard that.
And our only beauty is that we don't want a job. We don't want
a job there, in that system. We say to young people, "There is a
brilliant future for you in the revolution. Become an enemy of
the State. A great future. You will save your soul."

JUDGE HOFFMAN: The next defendant, Mr. Rubin, do you desire to speak in your own behalf? You have that privilege.

JERRY RUBIN: This is one of the proudest moments of my life. I
am happy because I know who I am. I am happy because I am
associated with Rennie, Tom, Dave, Abbie, and myself.

I'm being sentenced for five years not for what I did in Chicago—I did nothing in Chicago. I am going to jail because I am part of a historical movement and because of my life.

You see, you are not jailing five individuals. You are jailing a historical movement. We are symbols. You can just read the paper and see what is happening.

A father tells his son, "Respect me or else." That's what America told its youth. America told its youth, "Respect us or else." The kids grow up saying, "I am not going to respect you or else. When you are killing black people, I am not going to respect you."

We are on trial because we are trying to wake America up. We are on trial because we are trying to wake it up emotionally,

Jerry Rubin

because it turned us all into machines, it turned us all into marshals, reporters, judges, prosecutors; it's destroyed our humanity.

Judge, I want to give you a copy of this book [*Jerry Rubin's* Do It! Scenarios of the Revolution, *which had just been published*]. I want you to read it on your vacation in Florida, because this is why I am on trial. I inscribed it "Julius, you radicalized more young people than we ever could. You're the country's top Yippie."

You are jailing your youth, America. That's what you are doing. You are jailing your youth. And you are jailing it for the crime of dreaming, dreaming of an alternative. You are jailing it for the crime of idealism. Our crime is idealism. That's the only thing. And there is this slogan, you can jail the revolutionary but you can't jail a revolution.

What you are doing out there is creating millions of revolutionaries, millions of revolutionaries. Julius Hoffman, you have done more to destroy the court system in this country than any of us could have done. All we did was go to Chicago and the police system exposed itself as totalitarian.

This is the happiest moment of my life.

THE DEFENDANTS: RIGHT ON!

JUDGE HOFFMAN: I call on the Government to reply to the remarks of the defendants and each of them.

THOMAS FORAN: The Government has no comment on their remarks, your Honor. I think the evidence in the case speaks for itself.

JUDGE HOFFMAN: Mr. Clerk, the defendant David T. Dellinger will be committed to the custody of the Attorney General of the United States or his authorized representative for imprisonment for a term of five years. Further, the defendant Dellinger will be fined the sum of five thousand dollars and costs of prosecution, the defendant to stand committed until the fine and costs have been paid. That sentence of five years will be concurrent with the sentence the Court imposed for contempt of court previously. The two sentences will run concurrently.

Mr. Clerk, the defendant Rennard C. Davis will be committed to the custody of the Attorney General of the United States for a term of five years. Further a fine of—a fine will be imposed against Mr. Davis in the sum of five thousand dollars and costs of prosecution.

The defendant Thomas C. Hayden will be committed to the custody of the Attorney General of the United States for a term of five years. Further a fine of five thousand dollars and costs of prosecution will be imposed.

The defendant Abbott H. Hoffman will be committed to the custody of the Attorney General of the United States for a term of five years. Further a fine of five thousand dollars and costs—

ABBIE HOFFMAN: Five thousand dollars, judge? Could you make that three-fifty?

JUDGE HOFFMAN: Five thousand dollars and—

ABBIE HOFFMAN: How about three and a half?

JUDGE HOFFMAN: —and costs will be imposed, costs of prosecution will be imposed.

The defendant Jerry C. Rubin will be committed to the custody of the Attorney General of the United States for a term of five years. Further there will be a fine of five thousand dollars and costs of prosecution will be imposed.

William Kunstler

Not only on the record in this case, covering a period of four months or longer, but from the remarks made by the defendants themselves here today, the Court finds that the defendants are clearly dangerous persons to be at large. Therefore the commitments here will be without bail.

Does the Defense have any observations?

WILLIAM KUNSTLER: In conclusion, your Honor, speaking both for Mr. Weinglass and myself, we didn't need to hear our clients speak today to understand how much they meant to us but, after listening to them a few moments ago, we know that what they have said here has more meaning and will be longer remembered than any words said by us or by you.

JUDGE HOFFMAN: I gave you an opportunity to speak at the very beginning. You said counsel did not desire to speak.

WILLIAM KUNSTLER: Your Honor, couldn't I say my last words without cutting me off?

JUDGE HOFFMAN: You said you didn't want to speak.

WILLIAM KUNSTLER: Your Honor, I just said a moment ago we had a concluding remark. Your Honor has succeeded perhaps in sullying it, and I think that maybe that is the way the case should end, as it began.

Afterword

Tom Hayden

None of us were raised as conspirators. We grew up in the fifties void, when McCarthyism seemed to have eradicated any trace of subversion from American culture. We were radicalized when our youthful dreams of reform encountered a systemic pattern of violent response. In the Chicago Conspiracy trial, McCarthyism was resurrected once again, this time to fail. Times had changed.

I was a student editor of the campus newspaper at the University of Michigan when I began writing about the nonviolent direct-action campaign against racial segregation by Southern black students. Nonconformist by nature, I lacked any concrete political beliefs beyond an understanding that America's democratic promise was for everyone. As a reporter I had been arrested, beaten, jailed, and run out of Southern counties by a chain-swinging mob by the time I was twenty-one. When I met with Justice Department officials to plead for protection, I was told that civil rights workers in Mississippi couldn't be defended by their own federal government. Later I was arrested as a Freedom Rider for complying with federal law in southwest Georgia. And so it continued in Newark from 1964 to 1967, when I witnessed firsthand a culture of police brutality and investigated twenty-six deaths in the July 1967 riots, including that of a nineteen-year-old with forty-two shots to the head and upper torso, and in North Vietnam, where I interviewed peasants, women, and children wounded forever by U.S. fragmentation bombs. As idealism waned, a violent resentment filled my heart. As Albert Camus wrote of his experience in the French resistance, "seeing beloved friends and relatives killed is not a schooling in generosity. The temptation of hatred had to be overcome."

We were on our own. My father stopped talking to me, my mother couldn't understand me. She confused Indochina with Indonesia. To protest the war meant breaking their hearts. While my parents and the Catholic Church raised me to conform, I was anti-authority on some primal and instinctive level. At first there were editorials, then petitioning, then community organizing, then marching, then civil disobedience. Innocent blood kept spilling to achieve reforms long overdue, like equal treatment at a Woolworth's lunch counter, or voting rights legislation in 1965 after the deaths in Mississippi and the bloody Selma march. Yet Vietnam continued, claiming hundreds of American lives every week by 1968—and who knew how many Vietnamese, Cambodians, or Laotians? We who could be drafted could not vote for or against the politicians who sent us to Vietnam.

I was twenty-eight years old during the August 1968 Chicago protests, twenty-nine when the Conspiracy trial began. I felt that my life would be taken away, either by ten years behind bars, as our lawyers advised, or taken more literally. I considered going underground. Something enabled me to believe that if we could convince one good juror to vote for our acquittal—in legal terms, to nullify the prosecution—we could be vindicated by the kind of civil disobedience within the court system that we carried out by marching in the streets despite the unjust suspension of permits in Chicago 1968. In the end, we narrowly failed, because four jurors who thought we were completely innocent nevertheless compromised under pressure from the prosecution, finding five of us guilty of one felony count each. Bobby Seale had been found in contempt by the judge, and the remaining two were found innocent of all charges.

There was much talk at the time, even among blue-ribbon commissions, about a "youth crisis." Looking back, I believe it was more a "crisis of the elders" that was responsible for the trial and the events of the sixties. I also believe that the parents and grandparents of today, who came of age in the sixties, must remain faithful today to the way we were and not repeat the shortcomings of our own parents. Without elders, the past has no form.

There always was an Other America, whose heritage the Chicago Conspiracy rescued from oblivion. (Remember that Howard Zinn's *A People's History of the United States*, which reclaimed the radical tradition, was first published ten years after the Conspiracy trial, in 1980.) Before Bobby Seale and the Black Panther Party there were Nat Turner, Denmark Vesey, Harriet Tubman, Sojourner Truth, and the Underground Railroad. Before the Weather Underground (which exploded during the trial) there were the Haymarket anarchists, the Wobblies, the Mollie Maguires, and John Brown. Before Dave Dellinger there were the Quakers of New England and nonviolent saints like Dorothy Day and Rosa Parks. Before Rennie Davis, Lee Weiner, and John Froines there were the abolitionists, Henry David Thoreau, and the American populists and progressives. Before the Yippies there were the Diggers and Levellers, and Thomas Morton's revelers at Merry Mount, praised by Nathaniel Hawthorne and arrested by Captain Miles Standish.[1] I personally took heart from the lonely life of Thomas Paine. And, of course, our main lawyers, William Kunstler and Leonard Weinglass, stood in the tradition of lawyers like Clarence Darrow. As the historian Staughton Lynd tried to testify at the trial (he was rejected by the prosecution), the Chicago Eight were similar to the rebels at the 1770 Boston Massacre, described by none other than John Adams, lawyer for the British soldiers, as "a motley rabble of saucy boys, negroes, and molattoes, Irish taigs and outlandish jack tarrs."[2] Abbie Hoffman went even deeper into historical identity during the trial, for example, when he testified that he resided in "the Woodstock Nation," which he described as a "state of mind" like that of an Indian tribe. At trial's end, Abbie told the judge that he knew the patriots whose pictures hung on the courtroom wall: "I played with Sam Adams on the Concord Bridge. I was there when Paul Revere rode right up on his motorcycle and said, 'The pigs are coming, the pigs are coming.' "

This Other America, never triumphal but never defeated, once again rose in the sixties. Millions of young people, and some (but not many) of our parents, were on the march. They were riveted by the Chicago demonstrations and subsequent trial—a larger "jury," if you will, whose verdict of rage was delivered in the streets on the day we were convicted, when there were dozens of riots, and one bank burning in sunny Santa Barbara. Chicago not only radicalized many Americans, it also awakened a liberal conscience in response to the perceived outrages of the Nixon years.

The lesson for me was that some of us gave up on America prematurely. The Chicago Conspiracy was acquitted on appeal, four years after the trial. Many outsiders of 1968 became Democratic Party insiders by 1972. The law-and-order Republicans of the Nixon era were impeached or imprisoned just five years later. The Vietnam War, which Congress almost unanimously authorized in 1964, ended when Congress cut off funding ten years later. Heading into a downward spiral of chaos, the system stabilized itself by a surge of reforms: ending the draft, enfranchising eighteen-year-olds, reforming the presidential primaries, passing the War Powers Act and environmental laws, and the rest. The 1969 Woodstock Festival and the great Vietnam Moratorium both occurred at the very time that the Chicago trial was meant to chill dissent. It wasn't the revolution we imagined, nor was it the repression we feared. It was both real reform and a return to pacified stability.

But the human losses outweighed the gains. Two million Vietnamese, Cambodians, and Laotians were estimated dead, millions more wounded or displaced. Fifty-eight thousand dead Americans, many more wounded, disabled by Agent Orange, emotionally drained. Hundreds of billions of dollars wasted that could have been invested in ghettos, barrios, schools, and habitat preservation. Wars came and went to dispel the "Vietnam syndrome" and replace it once again with what Robert J. Lifton has called a Superpower Syndrome. Conservative cultural counteroffensives were launched to launder the stains of the sixties from the robes of re-proclaimed innocence. The sixties are fifty years old and still contested.

There are important reverberations of the sixties today in the recent movements against the Iraq War, corporate globalization, and curtailing of civil liberties. Back in the day, Attorney General John Mitchell declared, "We are going to take this country so far to the right you won't even recognize it." Instead of putting protestors in detention camps (the idea of his assistant, Richard Kleindienst), Mitchell went to jail himself amidst the Watergate scandal that terminated the conservatives' dream of repelling the sixties legacy. It would take three decades, culture wars, Contra wars, an (arguably) stolen election, and suicide attacks on New York and Washington before their opportunity to push rightward returned with the invasion of Iraq and passage of the Patriot Act.

The new cycle of radical protest began even before the Iraq War, with the "battle of Seattle" in 1999, which, like the opening of the sixties, caught the authorities and the media entirely by surprise. I was in the California state senate at the time, concerned about the threat of the World Trade Organization to California's laws on clean water, clean air, endangered species, and minority-owned and women-owned business preferences, all subject to challenge as "barriers" to the free-trade doctrines of the multinational corporations. But I was unaware of the rising intensity of resistance to the WTO among a new generation of young people. I received a call from a Yale student, Terra Lawson Remer, the daughter of sixties friends of mine, urging me not to miss Seattle. Then calls came from Michael Dolan, the Public Citizen coordinator, wanting me to speak as an "old-timer" at a kickoff rally. "Seattle," like "Chicago," became a single-word summary of a new historic event. It had happened before, in the general strike of the thirties, the Wobbly campaigns before then, all the way back to the naming of the city for Chief Seattle, there had been repeated cycles of action and apathy, meaning and forgetting.

Comparisons between Seattle 1999 and Chicago 1968 are useful. The Seattle protest was not only larger than Chicago by tenfold but was based on an alliance between street radicals, environmentalists, and organized labor never achieved in the sixties. Seattle actually *shut down* the secret and undemocratic WTO ministerial meeting, going beyond the resistance actions of the sixties. The spirit was the same. More women were involved in leadership. The affinity groups, born of necessity in Chicago, were far more sophisticated in Seattle, augmented by cell phones, mountain-climbing gear, and couriers on high-speed bikes.

One major difference was that Seattle exploded unexpectedly out of a context of a surface calm, while Chicago seemed to be the culmination of a near-decade of escalating resistance on many fronts. The word on Seattle among cynics and administration defenders was that it was "isolated."

But it seems to me that *the Seattle phenomenon has been a slow-moving Chicago.* Far from isolated, Seattle-type events keep occurring in places as diverse as Quebec City, Genoa, Cancún, Porto Alegre, and eventually at the gates of American political conventions. There was another parallel, too: as the sixties movements began in the segregated South and vaulted into the campus and antiwar movements, so these new movements began in the global "South" and grew into a broad resistance movement against economic and military empire. And even before the events of September 11, 2001, "Seattle" had become the pretext for a new politics of law-and-order instead of an occasion for America's elders to rethink their system of power.

In 2000 in Los Angeles, in a scenario quite like Chicago, the FBI, the police, the Secret Service, and the mayor warned that up to 70,000 "anarchists" representing "another Seattle" would descend on the Democratic national convention. In 1968, the same federal agencies, plus the Chicago police, issued warnings of black uprisings, hippie anarchy, free-love festivals, and LSD in the city water supply, all designed to frighten the public, discredit the antiwar protests, and justify preemptive measures like the denial of routine permits for marches, concerts, and sleeping in public parks. A side benefit was the opportunity for a bonanza in public funds for law enforcement to stockpile rubber bullets, pepper-spray launchers, and surveillance equipment in the event of future urban "disorders." In addition, going beyond Chicago, the Los Angeles authorities began constructing fenced-in "protest zones," topped with concertina wire, pens that were suited to their cramped vision of free expression.

Of course the projections always were wildly inflated. Instead of 70,000 anarchists in Los Angeles, there were some five to ten thousand homegrown activists, approximately the same number who turned up at the height of Chicago. There was virtually no disruption by protestors, except briefly on the first night when police forcibly shut down a fenced-in concert by

Rage Against the Machine, firing rubber bullets and gas grenades into the crowd after two or three black-clad anarchists started scaling a fence hundreds of yards from the convention site. My son Troy, then twenty-eight (the same age I was during Chicago), was shot and wounded on the wrist by one of the hundreds of "less than lethal" bullets fired that night. It could have blinded or killed him, as we shall see.

The same pattern has played itself out periodically during the past five years, with police making inflated and irresponsible predictions prior to official events such as Republican and Democratic conventions (2000, 2004), a WTO ministerial in Cancún (2002), and the Free Trade Agreement of the Americas meeting in Miami (2003); imposing severe restrictions on the First Amendment; raiding apartments without warrants; infiltrating undercover provocateurs and spies into peaceful protest groups; and doctoring their own videos to suppress evidence, while all the time collecting tens of millions in public funds for high-tech weaponry.

Police behavior at the conventions of 2004 far surpassed or equaled the 1968 Chicago police tactics, but with one exception: the police had learned not to beat young people bloody on television as they did in 1968. While there were exceptions—police overkill in Oakland on April 7, 2003, and New York City on April 27 of the same year, gassing was a constant, some beatings were administered in Seattle, a protestor was run over and killed in Genoa—the police had devised forms of control less shocking to the eye. For instance, fishnets were routinely used to scoop up scores of flailing protestors (and unlucky pedestrians) in New York, instead of vivid scenes of club-swinging police wading into crowds to make arrests. Though fewer skulls were cracked on camera, the main policy change was in public relations. Violence was rendered less visible. Plastic flexicuffs still could bind ankles to wrists; demonstrators could be held in special buses for twelve or eighteen hours, blinded with pepper spray, denied toilets, food, and water.[3]

From Seattle 1999 to New York 2004, another lesson of the Chicago Conspiracy trial was adopted by the authorities: while useful to magnify the anarchist threat before the official event, there should be no federal conspiracy trials afterward. There was a partial exception in the case of John Sellers, Ruckus Society coordinator, during the 2000 Republican convention in Philadelphia, but charges were dropped. The government has learned to avoid public spectacles like the Chicago trial if at all possible. Protesters have turned the tables with successful litigation against the police in Oakland and New York City over the 2003 incidents. The exceptions are important, however. The never-ending drug war, largely a continued backlash against the sixties counterculture, proceeds to incarcerate millions, despite public support for decriminalization and medical marijuana. Second, the sweeps and prosecutions against alleged Muslim terrorists are publicized to feed the public's anxiety, but even these cases have received critical responses at home and abroad. Managing the perception of terror, which would seem easier than the earlier task of repressing antiwar activists, proved too much for Attorney General John Ashcroft. Alongside its fear of hidden terrorists, the public still maintains a suspicion of government prosecutors rooted in the sixties and revived by the intelligence scandals over weapons of mass destruction.

Instead of imposing conspiracy charges after an event, a new approach is to preempt or chill mass demonstrations by silently deploying FBI agents to interrogate, even subpoena, political activists in their hometowns before they decide to attend events like political conventions. In 2002, the homeland security agency issued an all-points bulletin to investigate anyone with an "expressed dislike of attitudes and decisions of the U.S. government," and warn them that withholding information about civil disobedience is punishable.[4] In 2003, federal prosecutors subpoenaed Drake University for information on organizers of a peace forum.[5] In the same year, the FBI circulated a memo to all police departments to investigate and report suspicious activities.[6] Under the pretext of preventing another Seattle or 9/11, this was the revival of the sixties' counterintelligence programs all over again, if indeed they were ever terminated.

For months leading up to the Republican convention of 2004 in New York City, the police claimed as usual to have "secret" intelligence about subversive plots, none of which materialized. A massive law-enforcement buildup thus was justified, including a huge mechanical contraption said to emit a shrieking sound so piercing that demonstrators all around would collapse in quaking disorientation. The machine was aimed directly at demonstrators but not turned on, thus legitimized as a deterrent without a murmur of official concern. As in Chicago, routine permits were denied for mass rallies, even one many miles from the convention in the Great Lawn in Central Park. It was said that the grass would be disturbed by marching feet. Three times as many protestors were arrested in New York City—1,821—than during Chicago, the largest number ever at an American political convention. As of this writing, almost all the cases have been dropped for lack of evidence or resulted in acquittals. The New York security forces pocketed approximately $100 million for their security expenses. They escaped with little public embarrassment, except the convention-eve handcuffing of eighty-six-year-old Mike Wallace for double-parking and being "overly assertive."[7] Like a few others of us, Wallace had covered the 1968 Chicago convention, where he was punched on the chin and threatened with arrest on the convention floor.[8] Further documents and forensic analysis were released in December 2005, showing that New York undercover officers had instigated one of the week's only violent disruptions, as well as having arrested Rosario Dawson, who was filming a movie during the demonstrations.[9]

In Boston at the 2004 Democratic convention, there were virtually no demonstrators at all despite the usual predictions of chaos. The police still received more than $20 million in federal funds for a protest cage, surveillance cameras that they installed permanently in the ghetto, and the usual allotment of rubber bullets, pepper spray, and launchers. A few months later they used their new weaponry on college students partying the night of the Red Sox's World Series victory, killing a twenty-one-year-old woman, Victoria Snelgrove, with a direct shot in the eye from a pepper-spray pellet gun. Commenting on the Red Sox riots for the *New York Times*, the Seattle police chief said the aggressive new crowd-control techniques began with the 1999 Seattle demonstrations, which "really woke up the police."[10]

The ghost of John Mitchell must be smiling up from its undisclosed location. Despite the revival of vigorous democratic protest, the machinery of preemptive arrest and detention is being used on an experimental basis under the pretext of deterring terrorists. If and when there is another terrorist incident here—and the experts who are paid to protect us say that it's inevitable—one wonders what new limitations on freedom are prepared already.

Seattle symbolized the beginning of a new global movement for peace and justice not seen since 1968. The system is more flexible and cushioned than forty years ago. What was confined to the outside now is permitted on the inside. The media, as stenographers to the powerful, underplay or ignore those in the streets. But this new cycle of protest is not over, and—who knows—the new movements may come to far exceed those of my generation. I consider it a personal blessing to have experienced such movements twice in a lifetime.

Consider these comparisons:

- **Raw numbers.** The global justice movement, comparable to the sixties civil rights movement, generated crowds of 50,000 in Seattle, at least 100,000 in Quebec City and Genoa, and similar numbers at annual World Social Forums. The student anti-sweatshop movement has forced codes of conduct on some 128 universities and giant corporations, comparable to the apartheid divestment campaigns of the past. The global antiwar movement produced as many demonstrators in New York City and around the world *before* the March 2003 U.S. invasion—500,000 in New York—than the largest anti-Vietnam moratorium in 1969, which was then considered the largest demonstration in U.S. history.
- **Political impact.** While John Kerry's presidential campaign, with its flawed antiwar message, somewhat resembled that of Hubert Humphrey in 1968, the total number of antiwar voters, volunteers, paid organizers, and campaign contributors for Howard Dean alone far exceeded the resources given Senator Eugene McCarthy in 1968.

- **Consciousness of "the system."** Despite a powerful conservative constituency devoted to reversing the legacies of the sixties, surveys also show a majority concern about Iraq, empire, official deceit, corporate abuse, the environment, civil and women's rights, campaign-finance corruption, and institutional scandals not recorded since that earlier time. As the assassinations and CIA scandals of the sixties fed a public sense of shadowy conspiracies against democracy, so the recent controversies over stolen elections and fraudulent intelligence on Iraq have shaped a new generation's consciousness of a power elite where "high crimes and misdemeanors" seem routine.

- **The diffusion of progressive political power.** The Cold War left few alternatives to the American and Soviet-style behemoths. But the post–Cold War world has seen (former) revolutionaries come to power electorally in former U.S.-supported dictatorships like Bolivia, Brazil, Argentina, Uruguay, Chile, and South Africa, as well as the former Eastern bloc. The new post-dictatorship Latin American governments have been key allies with the new social movements in blocking the WTO and forcing consideration of a global New Deal. The impact of such social movements certainly was the crucial factor in pressuring European governments to stand up to the United States over Iraq during debates in the United Nations.

Though not reaching the crescendo of the late sixties, the new social movements have proven themselves in many ways more progressive, diverse, and inventive. As noted, women are in leadership everywhere. Tactics of resistance are more effec-

tive, disrupting institutions while maintaining a deep commitment to nonviolence. The hip-hop culture rivals, and may sur-
pass, the musicians and counterculture of times past. The
Internet-driven independent media is broader and more par-
ticipatory than was the underground press. Single issues seem
more easily woven into an agenda of the whole—empire versus
democracy, global standards of human rights, environmental
protection, living wages, corporate accountability—achieved
by the "people power" embodied in social movements and non-
governmental organizations, using both streets and the Inter-
net, to establish norms and enforceable treaties like Kyoto
(global warming), Cartagena (biodiversity), and the International Criminal Court, with or without the approval of the
hegemon in Washington.

I venture to guess that most, perhaps all, of the children of
the Chicago conspiracy have taken part in these recent movements since Seattle. My own son Troy, an actor and passionate
member of the hip-hop generation, was on the streets with
demonstrators in Seattle, Los Angeles, and New York. My
daughter Vanessa makes documentaries about needle exchange and is active in Moveon.org. Terra Lawson Remer,
whose father was in the underground media and whose mother
lived in a Berkeley commune and attended the Chicago trial,
was teargassed and jailed in the streets of Seattle and arrested
again for scaling a building to drop a "Bush Out" banner during
the 2004 New York convention. Vivian Rothstein, who was
handing out leaflets in Chicago's Grant Park in 1968, is the
mother of two young organizers in the labor movement among
immigrant workers in California today. Bob Ross, who helped
protect me from arrest in Chicago, is a university expert on

sweatshops and the global economy. Richard and Mickey Flacks, whose baby boy was teargassed in Chicago, have spent three decades teaching, writing, and building community organization. Such stories of continuity across generational lines are legion.

An interesting example is the rapid rise of Iraq veterans against the war and their military families, symbolized by Cindy Sheehan, who follow in the tradition of the Vietnam Veterans Against the War. One of their experienced leaders today is Army veteran Dave Cline, whose roots go back to a little-remembered drama during Chicago 1968. It was my thinking at the time that we might not only stop the controlled machinery of the Democratic Party with an inside-outside strategy, but also trigger a simultaneous revolt for peace within the armed forces. Dave Cline had recently returned from Vietnam and was stationed at Fort Hood, Texas, when orders came to prepare to occupy the streets of Chicago with 6,000 combat troops. For some while, activists had been organizing against the war around Fort Hood at a GI coffeehouse called Oleo Strut. When the orders for Chicago came down, many soldiers were wearing peace stickers on their helmets. Hundreds of black GIs held a mutinous meeting all night in a parking lot to decide what to do. Finally they were stormed by MPs with bayonets; several were beaten, and forty-three soldiers in all were eventually court-martialed. After eliminating the most obvious dissidents, the 6,000 were sent to Chicago, arriving in full armor with flamethrowers and bazookas. An Oleo Strut organizer was arrested before he could get to Chicago. In the assessment of researcher and documentary filmmaker David Zeiger, "They didn't use the Fort Hood troops [in Chicago] because they genuinely didn't trust them."

Thus we came close to an apocalyptic ending in Chicago, with a majority of delegates walking out of the convention to meet soldiers from Vietnam wearing peace stickers. In the end, over 1,000 delegates—more than 40 percent—voted for a Vietnam peace plank, and hundreds walked out to join the protests. The Fort Hood troops were never used for fear that some would point their weapons the wrong way. Even the mainstream media revolted; for example, NBC's Chet Huntley reported that "we in the calling of journalism have hesitated to talk about our problems in Chicago . . . but the hostility towards any kind of criticism, and the fear of telling how it is, has become too much and it becomes our duty to speak out."[11]

What the authorities cannot erase they will deface. There is a continuing battle of memory over Chicago. Let me briefly address some myths and identify some unknowns.

Myth number one: that we conspired to riot. Truth: most of the Chicago Eight didn't know each other. We always kept multiple scenarios in mind (if we received permits or not, for example), but expected the violence to be launched by the police. U.S. Attorney General Ramsey Clark, who had prosecuted draft resisters, chose not to indict any of us after the Chicago confrontations. That choice was left to the incoming Nixon administration.

Myth number two: the police "rioted." Truth: aside from countless acts of random police violence, there is plenty of evidence that the violence and intimidation were intentional. The commander of the National Guard "said his men would 'shoot to kill' . . . if there is no other way of preventing the commission of a forcible felony during the convention."[12] The City "attempted to discourage an inundation of demonstrators by not granting permits for marches and rallies," according to the

Walker Commission.[13] Police violence against the media was "plainly deliberate."[14] Police behavior in repressing the April 1968 riots after Dr. King's assassination was described as "ostentatious" by a blue-ribbon commission.[15] The unknown question is where in the chain of command the decisions were made. The FBI, intelligence agencies, and Chicago police met continuously from January to August 1968 to coordinate decisions. According to a J. Edgar Hoover memo of October 23, 1968, "A successful prosecution of this type would be a unique achievement of the Bureau and should seriously disrupt and curtail the activities of the New Left." Far from an overreaction by a few Chicago police officers, the behavior of the security forces had an organized quality to it.

Myth number three: the Conspiracy defendants planned a courtroom carnival of disruption. The truth, according to research by Chicago professor Harry Kalven, is that nearly all the contempt-of-court citations occurred during a few days in the five-month trial: the chaining and gagging of Bobby Seale, the jailing of Dave Dellinger for a speech. A retrial in 1973, conducted by a federal judge from Maine, threw out 146 of Judge Hoffman's contempt findings. The logic of the trial paralleled the logic of 1968. To the extent that the judge suspended our courtroom rights, for instance by denying Bobby Seale a counsel of his choice, we affirmed a right to dissent, including the right to call on the jury to nullify the law itself. There was an inner logic, including an unorthodox legal logic, to the disruptions. They were not intended, to reinterpret Abbie's famous description of revolution, "for the hell of it." The unanswered question is what would have occurred under another judge, or if the court had allowed Charles Garry to represent Bobby Seale. As I asked the prosecutors, "If you didn't want to make us martyrs, why did you do it?"

Myth number four: the Conspiracy defendants were more radical and violent than the rest of our generation, the main argument of the prosecution. A 1969 Yankelovich survey found that 10 percent of American students—about one million—favored "a mass revolutionary party," while 69 percent considered themselves doves on Vietnam.[16] According to U.S. Treasury Department figures, there were thousands of bombings in the United States between January 1969 and April 1970, roughly the period of the Chicago trial. Beginning in 1969, there were 240 incidents of GIs fragging their officers per year, over 10 percent resulting in fatalities.

Since our 1968 revolt was dismissed as the "death rattle of the historical irrelevants" by Zbigniew Brzezinski,[17] then a Columbia professor and later U.S. national security advisor, one might ask: why is the Chicago Conspiracy trial so remembered, so debated still, the stuff of textbooks, films, and television specials like few other trials of the past hundred years?

The readers of these transcripts can judge for themselves. I think that our protests, symbolized by Chicago, threatened the arrangements of power more than at any time in fifty years, perhaps longer when considered globally. The trial touched a nerve and lodged in America's psyche.

There is a clue to this significance in an internal State Department document dated November 17, 1967. Three weeks earlier, some 100,000 protestors, among them Rennie Davis, defiantly surrounded the Pentagon, holding up a U.S.-made fragmentation bomb used on the Vietnamese people; Dave Dellinger, coordinating as ever; and the Yippies Abbie Hoffman and Jerry Rubin, who proclaimed their intent to "levitate" the building. First Lady Lady Bird Johnson wrote in her diary of "feeling under siege." [18] CIA director Richard Helms said, "I'd had experiences with mobs all over the world and I didn't like the look or sound of this one bit." [19] Sharpshooters were on the Pentagon roof. The president told his advisers, "They are not going to run me out of town," took nightly memos on the antiwar movement to bed, and contemplated resigning. [20]

In the aftermath of this unprecedented demonstration, analysts at State offered their observation in the November 17 memo: *"The policy priorities of youth may run counter to the requirements imposed on the US by its role as a world power."* [21]

Coming just weeks after the Democrats chose Chicago for their 1968 convention site, the 1967 Pentagon demonstrations became the main template for the plan for Chicago. We imagined 100,000 peace demonstrators would surround the convention amphitheater. Phil Ochs, Judy Collins, and Allen Ginsberg would lift their voices. The wagons of Martin Luther King Jr.'s Poor People's Campaign would roll in from Washington. Delegates on the inside would revolt against the party bosses and nominate a peace candidate. U.S. troops would resist orders to repress the demonstrations. All over the country, crowds would spontaneously hit the streets demanding immediate withdrawal from war and repression. That was the idea and, after the 1967 Pentagon demonstration, it was both credible and absolutely intolerable to the powers.

Of course what then happened from January to August was unprecedented: the murders of Martin Luther King Jr. and Robert Kennedy; the resignation of Lyndon Johnson; campus rebellions at Columbia and a hundred other universities;

strikes and uprisings in Germany, France, Mexico, Northern Ireland, and elsewhere; the shooting of German SDS leader Rudi Dutschke; black-power salutes by U.S. Olympic athletes; and the oddly coincidental Soviet invasion of Czechoslovakia. The times were radical. The prosecution that followed became an opportunity to suppress what the sixties had wrought, "to seriously disrupt and curtail the New Left," as Hoover had put it.

Ever since January 1962, when the U.S. government had established an internal group to monitor and influence student movements, the White House had been warned in memos that "we are not adequately attuned to the needs and desires of youth and youth groups in the free world and that we have no specific program directed towards capturing the minds of these individuals." [22] By mid-1968, the department had formed an internal "Student Unrest Study Group" to assess a global student movement that had "toppled prime ministers, changed governments, ruined universities and in some cases harmed the economy of the country . . . [through] a camaraderie with other students around the world who are doing the same thing." [23]

Instead of reforming the conditions leading to this revolutionary breakdown, undercover police acting on higher orders went on a crusade to "neutralize" the New Left. Concerning myself, J. Edgar Hoover sent out a secret memo on May 17, 1968, ordering that a prime FBI objective was to "neutralize [Hayden] in the New Left movement. The Bureau will entertain recommendations of a counter-intelligence nature in order to accomplish this objective." Sometimes it was ludicrous; one FBI memo stated that the "complete disregard for moral and social laws and amenities [such as 'neglect of personal cleanliness' and 'unusual jewelry'] "negate any attempt to hold these people up to ridicule." [24]

But only consider what happened to my world in that brief springtime. Martin Luther King Jr., whom I first interviewed in 1960, was murdered; Robert Kennedy, whose casket I stood beside, was shot in the head only weeks later. My close friend and SDS co-founder Richard Flacks suffered a fractured skull and slashed wrists from an unknown assailant in his University of Chicago office on May 5, at a time when FBI memos show a plot to have him fired. On May 15, I woke up to discover Berkeley police and state troopers, backed by a helicopter, invading People's Park, launching seventeen days of street fighting in which deputies fired double-O buckshot, killing one bystander and blinding another. This was not all: there came the 1970–71 Chicano moratoriums, with four dead and many wounded, and Kent State and Jackson State in 1970, with six more killed. Before the Chicago conventions were reversed, there would be the 1973 siege of Wounded Knee and the beating of Vietnam vets against the war. [25] It is hard to transmit this traumatic context to another generation nearly forty years later. But perhaps the passage of time makes the story easier to hear.

I am haunted by this question: are we members of the sixties generation, now the elders ourselves, still doing all we can to realize the dreams of our youth? The generational story is far from over, and this publication of excerpts from the Chicago trial transcripts, along with the painstaking history by Jon Wiener, is an important contribution to the intergenerational dialogue we must have.

For myself, I offer what I wrote forty years ago in the *New Republic* magazine:

> Is the only value in rebellion itself, in the countless momentary times when people transcend their pettiness to commit themselves to great purposes? If so, then radicalism is doomed to be extraordinary, erupting only during those rare times of crisis and upsurge which American elites seem able to ride.
>
> The alternative, if there is one, might be for radicalism to make itself ordinary, patiently taking up work that has only the virtue of facing and becoming part of the realities which are society's secrets and its disgrace. . . .
>
> Radicalism would then give itself to, and become part of, the energy that is kept restless and active under the clamps of a paralyzed imperial society. Radicalism then would go beyond the concepts of optimism and pessimism as guides to work, finding itself in working despite the odds. Its realism and sanity would be grounded in nothing more than the ability to face whatever comes.

Notes

Introduction: The Sixties on Trial

1. David Farber, *Chicago '68* (Chicago: University of Chicago Press, 1988), xiii.
2. This volume, 101.
3. Jonah Raskin, *For the Hell of It: The Life and Times of Abbie Hoffman* (Berkeley: University of California Press, 1996), 118.
4. This volume, 159.
5. Quoted in Raskin, *For the Hell of It*, 118.
6. Tom Hayden, *Reunion: A Memoir* (New York: Random House, 1988), 348.
7. J. Anthony Lukas, *The Barnyard Epithet and Other Obscenities: Notes on the Chicago Conspiracy Trial* (New York: Harper & Row, 1970), 15.
8. Ibid., 14.
9. Ibid., 12.
10. Tom Hayden, *The Port Huron Statement: The Visionary Call of the 1960s Revolution* (New York: Thunder's Mouth Press, 2005).
11. For annual casualty figures see www.vietnamwall.org/casualty.html.
12. Hayden, *Reunion*, 304, 306.
13. Todd Gitlin, *The Sixties: Years of Hope, Days of Rage* (New York:

Bantam Books, 1987), 334. The mayor's statement was apparently too offensive to be quoted in the 1988 University of Chicago Press book by David Farber, *Chicago '68*—he writes euphemistically only that "off microphone, the Mayor cursed," 201. Eight years later, in 1996, the University of California Press book by Jonah Raskin, *For the Hell of It*, published the full quote: 166. It also appears in different forms in recent books intended for use in college classrooms: Mark Hamilton Lytle, *America's Uncivil Wars: The Sixties Era from Elvis to the Fall of Richard Nixon* (New York: Oxford University Press, 2006), 263, includes "fuck you, you Jew son of a bitch," but leaves out "you lousy motherfucker," while the full quote including "you lousy motherfucker" appears in Maurice Isserman and Michael Kazin, *America Divided: The Civil War of the 1960s* (New York: Oxford University Press, 2004), 242.

14. See for example Lytle, *America's Uncivil Wars*, 264.
15. Quoted in Lukas, *Barnyard Epithet*, 49, 50.
16. Ibid., 87.
17. On conspiracy law, see Jason Epstein, *The Great Conspiracy Trial: An Essay on Law, Liberty and the Constitution* (New York: Random House, 1970).
18. Quoted in Lukas, *Barnyard Epithet*, 73.
19. Clay Carson, "The Cambridge Convergence: How a Night in Maryland 30 Years Ago Changed the Nation's Course of Racial Politics," *Minneapolis Star Tribune*, July 28, 1997, www .stanford.edu/group/King/about_the_project/ccarson/articles/ cambridge_convergence.htm.
20. Quoted in Lytle, *America's Uncivil Wars*, 234.
21. Quoted in Carson, "The Cambridge Convergence."
22. Ibid.
23. Quoted in Epstein, *Great Conspiracy Trial*, 43.
24. Quoted in Epstein, *Great Conspiracy Trial*, 52–53.
25. Ramsey Clark, "Preface," in *Contempt: Transcript of the Contempt Citations, Sentences, and Responses of the Chicago Conspiracy 10* (Chicago: Swallow Press, 1970), v–viii.

26. Ibid., vi.
27. Ibid., vii.
28. Ibid.
29. Hayden, *Reunion*, 381.
30. Ibid., 405.
31. Ibid., 406.
32. Ibid., 407.
33. John Schultz, *The Chicago Conspiracy Trial* (Cambridge, MA.: Da Capo Press, 1993), 366–68.
34. See *Contempt; Conspiracy on Appeal: Appellate Brief on Behalf of the Chicago Eight* (New York: Center for Constitutional Rights, 1971).
35. Harry Kalven, introduction to *Contempt*, xviii–xix.
36. Judge Julius Hoffman died at age eighty-eight on July 1, 1983.
37. Raskin, *For the Hell of It*, 224; Abbie Hoffman, *Soon to Be a Major Motion Picture* (New York: Putnam, 1980), 294, 205.
38. Quoted in Raskin, *For the Hell of It*, 241.
39. Quoted in ibid., 255.
40. Quoted in ibid., 252.
41. Ibid., 258.
42. Hayden, *Reunion*, 462.
43. en.wikipedia.org/wiki/Prem_Rawat
44. James Moore, "Rennie Davis: From Chicago 7 to Venture Capitalist to Grand Canyon Visionary," *Iowa Source*, March 2005, www.iowasource.com/conscious_living/conscious_living_rennie _0305.html
45. venturesforhumanity.net/
46. Jerry Rubin, *Do It!* (New York: Simon & Schuster, 1970), back cover.
47. Jerry Rubin, *Growing (Up) at 37* (New York: Warner Books, 1976), 197.
48. Eric Pace, "Jerry Rubin, 1960's Radical and Yippie Leader, Dies at 56," *New York Times*, November 29, 1994.
49. David Dellinger, *From Yale to Jail: The Life Story of a Moral Dissenter* (New York: Pantheon Books, 1993), 401–4.

50. David Dellinger, "Hungering for Real U.S. Issues," *Los Angeles Times,* September 30, 1992, quoted in Dellinger, *From Yale to Jail,* 478–80.

51. Michael Carlson, "David Dellinger: Pacifist Elder Statesman of the Anti-Vietnam Chicago Eight," *The Guardian* (London), May 28, 2004, www.guardian.co.uk/antiwar/story/0,12809,1226643,00.html.

52. Edward Jay Epstein, "The Black Panthers and the Police: A Pattern of Genocide?" *New Yorker,* February 13, 1971, www.edwardjayepstein.com/archived/panthers2.htm; UC Berkeley Library Social Activism Sound Recording Project: The Black Panther Party, www.lib.berkeley.edu/MRC/pacificapanthers.html; "Black Panther Party," in *Africana Civil Rights: An A-Z Reference,* ed. Kwame Anthony Appiah and Henry Louis Gates Jr. (Philadelphia: Running Press, 2000), 79–81.

53. UC Berkeley Library project, ibid.

54. Edward Jay Epstein, "Black Panthers and the Police," ibid.

55. "Bobby Seale," in *Africana Civil Rights,* 363.

56. Hayden, *Reunion,* 471.

57. Dan Walters, *Sacramento Bee,* quoted at www.thenation.com/directory/bios/tom_hayden.

58. Tom Hayden, "An Exit Strategy for Iraq Now," *Los Angeles Times,* August 18, 2005, B7.

The Government Case

1. Tom Hayden, *Reunion: A Memoir* (New York: Random House, 1988), 345.

2. Ibid., 368–69.

3. Ibid., 369.

4. Ibid., 371.

5. Ibid., 374.

6. Ibid., 380.

The Case for the Defense

1. Tom Hayden, *Reunion: A Memoir* (New York: Random House, 1988), 381.
2. Jason Epstein, *The Great Conspiracy Trial: An Essay on Law, Liberty and the Constitution* (New York: Random House, 1970), 320.
3. Editorial, *New York Times*, February 1, 1970, quoted in Hayden, *Reunion*, 393.
4. Hayden, *Reunion*, 382.

Afterword

1. Peter Lamborn Wilson, "Caliban's Masque: Spiritual Anarchy and the Wild Man in Colonial America," in *Gone to Croatan: Origins of North American Dropout Culture*, ed. Ron Sakolsky and James Koehnline (Brooklyn, NY: Autonomedia, 1993), 95.
2. Howard Zinn, *A People's History of the United States* (New York: HarperCollins, 2003), 67.
3. See Carolyn Marshall, "Oakland Nears Final Payouts for Protesters Hurt by Police," *New York Times*, March 20, 2006, A14; National Lawyers Guild summary, "The Assault on Free Speech, Public Assembly and Dissent," August 2003; Lewis Lapham, "Crowd Control," *Harper's*, October 2004.
4. Lapham, "Crowd Control."
5. Eric Lichtblau, "F.B.I. Goes Knocking for Political Troublemakers," *New York Times*, August 16, 2004.
6. Ibid.
7. James Barron, "Incident Puts Taxi Officers in Spotlight," *New York Times*, August 12, 2004.
8. Daniel Walker, *Rights in Conflict: A Report to the National Commission on the Causes and Prevention of Violence* (New York: Dutton, 1968), 327. Lest anyone be mistaken in thinking that Mike Wallace was a liberal sympathizer, he met with me a few weeks after the convention to propose that I support Richard Nixon. "Tom, believe me, he's a 'new Nixon,' " Wallace confided. I passed.

9. Jim Dwyer, "New York Police Covertly Join in at Protest Rallies," *New York Times*, December 22, 2005.

10. Fox Butterfield, "Student's Death Returns Crowd Control to the Fore," *New York Times*, November 1, 2004.

11. Walker, *Rights in Conflict*, 322.

12. *Chicago Daily News*, August 25, 1968.

13. Walker, *Rights in Conflict*, 2.

14. Ibid., 7.

15. Sparling Commission, cited by Dave Dellinger in Abbie Hoffman et al., *The Conspiracy* (New York: Dell, 1969), 141.

16. Todd Gitlin, *The Sixties: Years of Hope, Days of Rage* (New York: Bantam Books, 1987).

17. Zbigniew Brzezinski, in the essay "Revolution and Counter-Revolution," cited in David Farber, *Chicago '68* (Chicago: University of Chicago Press, 1988), 238.

18. Cited in Jonathan Neale, *A People's History of the Vietnam War* (New York: The New Press, 2003), 132–33.

19. Ibid., 133.

20. David Maraniss, *They Marched into Sunlight: War and Peace, Vietnam and America, October 1967* (New York: Simon & Schuster, 2003), 191, 314.

21. Martin Klimke, " 'A Serious Concern of US Foreign Policy': The West German Student Movement and the Western Alliance," paper given at the University of Heidelberg conference on "The Other Alliance," May 19–22, 2005; original State Department document "Youth and Revolt—Depth and Diversity" in RG 59, IAYC Records, IAYC meeting, November 8, 1967, Box 1.

22. Undersecretary of State George McGee, "Goals for Free World Youth," January 23, 1962, University of Arkansas Special Collections, in Klimke, " 'A Serious Concern of US Foreign Policy,' " 3.

23. George McGee to President Johnson, in McGee papers, Georgetown University, in Klimke, " 'A Serious Concern of US Foreign Policy,' " 2.

24. FBI memorandum, May 27, 1968.

25. For example, during the Chicano movement, an FBI infiltrator

confessed that federal and local law enforcement directed him to
" 'cause confusion . . . [and] provoke incidents' in order 'to elimi-
nate' the Brown Berets and the NCMC [the National Chicano
Moratorium Committee]." See F. Arturo Rosales, *Chicano! The
History of the Mexican American Civil Rights Movement* (Houston,
TX: Arté Publico Press, 1997); original in Edward J. Escobar,
"The Dialectics of Repression: The Los Angeles Police Depart-
ment and the Chicano Movement, 1968–71," *Journal of American
History* 79 (March 1993): 1505.